The Narrative of the
CAPTIVITY
and
RESTORATION
of
MRS. MARY ROWLANDSON

FIRST PRINTED in 1682 at CAMBRIDGE,
Massachusetts, & LONDON, *England*

Whereunto are annexed
A *Map* of her *Removes* & *Biographical* & *Historical*
Notes

THE LANCASTER TERCENTENARY EDITION

REPRINTED
SANDWICH, MASSACHUSETTS
CHAPMAN BILLIES, INCORPORATED

ISBN 0-939218-20-8

Printed in the United States of America

This edition of
The Narrrative of the Capture and Restoration of
Mrs. Mary Rowlandson is a reprint of one
published in Lancaster, Massachusetts, in 1953.

It is published by Chapman Billies, Inc.
and distributed by Alan C. Hood & Co., Inc.
P.O. Box 775, Chambersburg, PA 17201

"I am confident that no Friend of divine Providence will ever repent his time and pains, spent in reading over these sheets, but will judge them worth perusing again and again."

Preface to the Second Edition, 1682

PREFACE

LANCASTER was incorporated as a town on May 18, 1653 by the General Court of the Massachusetts Bay Colony. In October, 1653, the town orders and covenant of the present First Church of Christ in Lancaster had been signed by twenty-seven heads of families of the town, and by 1660 fifty-four had subscribed.*

The celebration of the Three Hundredth Anniversary of town and church is therefore a fitting time for the republication of the Narrative of Captivity written by Mary Rowlandson, the devout helpmate of Lancaster's first ordained minister. While her simply told tale was the earliest literary composition by a citizen of this town to win the distinction of print, it is also an invaluable contribution to early New England history. It presents a first hand, contemporary picture of Indian life and customs. It is an eloquent record of grave perils bravely encountered, and terrible sufferings patiently borne with an unswerving faith in the wisdom and mercy of an overruling Providence.

First issued from the press in 1682, it at once commanded attention in Old as well as in New England. No book of its period can boast equal evidence of enduring public favor with this work of a

*(Nourse: *Early Records of Lancaster*, 1643–1725, Lancaster, 1884, pp. 30–31).

young Lancaster wife and mother, who had spent twenty-three of her thirty-eight years in this town; and very few books in any age or tongue, if we except the masterpieces of literature, have been distinguished with more editions. Thirty-eight reprints attest the popular interest in this modest story of personal experience. Of the first edition, no copy is known to exist; only a few copies of the other early editions have survived; even a copy of one of the many later editions is now so rare as to command a considerable price at book auctions. The Lancaster Collection of the Lancaster Town Library possesses perhaps the finest collection of these editions including a copy of nearly every existing reprint.

The present edition (1953) is derived from the rudely printed and badly damaged copy once belonging to the Reverend John Cotton, Jr., now preserved in the Prince Collection of the Boston Public Library. When the Lancaster edition of 1930 was published, from which the present copy is reproduced, Mr. John Eliot Thayer generously allowed the undersigned, as editor, to make abridgments of the notes and to use illustrations from the scholarly edition which he and Mr. Henry Stedman Nourse published in 1903, and these are again used here. To this is appended the Map of Removes taken from the same source. The spelling and punctuation have been modernized, but the text adheres to the edition of 1682.

LANCASTER
May 18, 1953   FREDERICK LEWIS WEIS

ILLUSTRATIONS

This piece of household furniture, of solid English oak, is supposed to have been brought to New England and to Lancaster, by John White, the father of Mary Rowlandson. After the division of John White's personal estate it probably fell to the Rowlandsons. The story is that it contained valuables and was removed by the Indians from the burning house and ransacked. Later the Rowlandsons apparently had it in Weathersfield, Connecticut, and the line of descent has been traced and authenticated. It was bought by the library in Lancaster in 1876 for the sum of $100, and it is now valued at between $10,000 and $15,000.

The cut on the cover is reproduced from the title-page of the 1773 edition of the *Narrative* published in Boston 'at John Boyle's Printing-Office, next Door to the *Three Doves* on Marlborough-Street.'

The Narrative of the
CAPTIVITY
and
RESTORATION
of
MRS. MARY ROWLANDSON

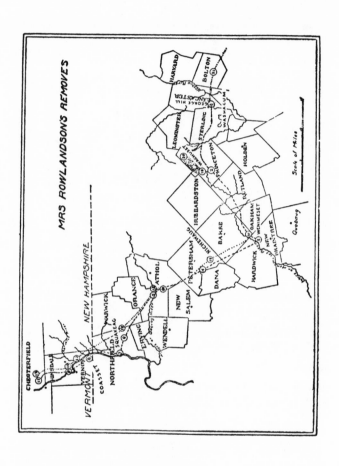

MRS ROWLANDSON'S REMOVES

The Narrative of the
CAPTIVITY
and
RESTORATION
of
Mrs. Mary Rowlandson

ON the tenth of February, 1675,[1] came the Indians in great numbers upon Lancaster. Their first coming was about sun-rising. Hearing the noise of some guns, we looked out: several houses were burning, and the smoke ascending to heaven. There were five persons [2] taken in one house; the father, the mother, and a suckling child they knocked on the head; the other two they took and carried away alive. There were two others, who being out of their garrison upon some occasion, were set upon; one was knocked on the head, the other escaped. Another there was, who, running along, was shot and wounded, and fell down; he begged of them his life, promising them money, (as they told me,) but they would not hearken

[1] "February 10, 1675/6" (February 20, 1676, New Style), fell upon Thursday.

[2] This was the family of John Ball, the tailor. His home was on the slope of the George Hill range.

to him, but knocked him in head, and stripped him naked, and split open his bowels. Another, seeing many of the Indians about his barn, ventured and went out, but was quickly shot down. There were three others belonging to the same garrison [3] who were killed; the Indians getting up upon the roof of the barn, had advantage to shoot down upon them over their fortification. Thus these murderous wretches went on burning and destroying [all] before them.

At length they came and beset our own house, and quickly it was the dolefulest day that ever mine eyes saw. The house stood upon the edge of a hill; [4] some of the Indians got behind the hill, others into the barn, and others behind any thing that would shelter them; from all which places they shot against the house, so that the bullets seemed to fly like hail; and quickly they wounded one man among us, then another, and then a third. About two hours (according to my observation in that amazing time) they had been about the house before they prevailed to fire it (which they did with flax and hemp which they brought out of the barn, there being no defence about the house, only two flankers at two opposite corners, and one of them not finished). They fired it once, and one ventured out and quenched it, but they

[3] This was the garrison of Richard Wheeler, probably on the south slope of George Hill, in South Lancaster.

[4] The minister's dwelling was west of the present Middle Cemetery and two or three rods down the slope from the present highway. The meeting-house stood upon the highest ground in the cemetery.

quickly fired it again, and that took. Now is the dreadful hour come, that I have often heard of (in time of war, as was the case with others) but now mine eyes see it. Some in our house were fighting for their lives, others wallowing in their blood, the house on fire over our heads, and the bloody heathen ready to knock us on the head if we stirred out. Now might we hear mothers and children crying out for themselves, and one another, *Lord, what shall we do?* Then I took my children (and one of my sisters her's) to go forth and leave the house: but as soon as we came to the door, and appeared, the Indians shot so thick, that the bullets rattled against the house, as if one had taken an handful of stones and threw them, so that we were fain to give back. We had six stout dogs belonging to our garrison, but none of them would stir, though [at] another time, if an Indian had come to the door, they were ready to fly upon him and tear him down. The Lord hereby would make us the more to acknowledge his hand, and to see that our help is always in him. But out we must go, the fire increasing, and coming along behind us, roaring, and the Indians gaping before us with their guns, spears, and hatchets, to devour us. No sooner were we out of the house, but my brother-in-law [5] (being before wounded, in defending the house, in or near the throat) fell down dead, whereat the Indians scornfully shouted,

[5] Ensign John Divoll commanded the garrison on the day of the massacre. His wife was Hannah, Mrs. Rowlandson's youngest sister.

and hallooed, and were presently upon him, stripping off his clothes. The bullets flying thick, one went through my side, and the same (as [it] would seem) through the bowels and hand of my dear child in my arms. One of my elder sister's children,[6] named William, had then his leg broken, which the Indians perceiving, they knocked him on the head. Thus were we butchered by those merciless heathens, standing amazed, with the blood running down to our heels. My elder sister being yet in the house, and seeing those woeful sights, the infidels hauling mothers one way, and children another, and some wallowing in their blood, and her eldest son telling her that her son William was dead, and myself was wounded, she said, And, *Lord let me die with them:* which was no sooner said, but she was struck with a bullet, and fell down dead over the threshold. I hope she is reaping the fruit of her good labors, being faithful to the service of God in her place. In her younger years she lay under much trouble upon spiritual accounts, till it pleased God to make that precious scripture take hold of her heart, 2 Cor. xii. 9. *And he said unto me, my grace is sufficient for thee.* More than twenty years after, I have heard her tell how sweet and comfortable that place was to her. But to return: the Indians laid hold of us, pulling me one way, and the children an-

----

[6] "My elder sister's children." Elizabeth was the wife of Lieutenant Henry Kerley. Her children were: Henry, born 1657; William, 1659; Elizabeth, *ca.* 1661; Hannah, 1663; Mary, 1666; Joseph, 1669; Martha, 1672.

other, and said, "Come, go along with us." I told them they would kill me. They answered, if I were willing to go along with them, they would not hurt me.

Oh! the doleful sight that now was to behold at this house! Come, behold the works of the Lord, what desolations he has made in the earth. Of thirty-seven persons [7] who were in this one house,

[7] "*Of thirty-seven persons*," etc. The contemporary historian, William Hubbard, gives *forty-two* as the number in the Rowlandson garrison. Daniel Gookin says "*about forty*." Other contemporary accounts give the total casualties as *fifty-five*. Mrs. Rowlandson may not have taken into account the soldiers from other places assigned to the garrisons who doubtless suffered loss. According to Treasurer Hull's accounts there were fourteen soldiers serving in the town on January 25. The following is a list of the victims known:

Killed in Rowlandson Garrison (11)
Ensign John Divoll; Josiah Divoll, son of John, aged 7; Daniel Gains; Abraham Joslin, aged 26; John MacLoud; Thomas Rowlandson, nephew of the minister, aged 19; Mrs. Elizabeth Kerley, wife of Lieutenant Henry; William Kerley, son of Lieutenant Henry, aged 17; Joseph Kerley, son of Lieutenant Henry, aged 7; Mrs. Priscilla Roper, wife of Ephraim; Priscilla Roper, child of Ephraim, aged 3.

Carried Captive from Rowlandson Garrison (20 + 1)
Mrs. Mary Rowlandson, wife of the minister, ransomed; Mary Rowlandson, daughter of the minister, aged 10, ransomed; Sarah Rowlandson, daughter of the minister, aged 6, wounded and died February 18; Joseph Rowlandson, son of the minister, aged 13, ransomed; Mrs. Hannah Divoll, wife of Ensign John, ransomed; John Divoll, son of Ensign John, aged 12, probably died a captive; William Divoll, son of Ensign John, aged 4, ransomed; Hannah Divoll, daughter of Ensign John, probably died a captive; Mrs. Ann Joslin, wife of Abraham, killed in captivity; Beatrice Joslin, daughter of Abraham, killed in captivity; Joseph Joslin, brother of

none escaped either present death, or a bitter
captivity, save only one, who might say as in
Job i. 15: And I only am escaped to tell the news.
There were twelve killed, some shot, some stabbed
with their spears, some knocked down with their
hatchets. When we are in prosperity, oh, the little
that we think of such dreadful sights, and to see our
dear friends and relations lie bleeding out their
heart's blood upon the ground. There was one who
was chopped into the head with a hatchet, and
stripped naked, and yet was crawling up and down.
It is a solemn sight to see so many Christians lying in
their blood, some here, and some there, like a com-

Abraham, aged 16; Henry Kerley, son of Lieutenant Henry, aged
18; Elizabeth Kerley, daughter of Lieutenant Henry, aged about
15; Hannah Kerley, her sister, aged 13; Mary Kerley, her sister,
aged 10; Martha Kerley, her sister, aged 4; Mrs. Elizabeth Kettle,
wife of John, ransomed; Sarah Kettle, daughter of John, aged 15,
escaped; Jonathan Kettle, her brother, aged 5; a child Kettle,
daughter of John. Ephraim Roper alone escaped during the
assault.

*Killed outside of Rowlandson Garrison, being all of South Lan-
caster* (11)
John Ball; Mrs. Elizabeth Ball, wife of John; an infant child of John
Ball; Jonas Fairbank; Joshua Fairbank, son of Jonas, aged 15;
Ephraim Sawyer, aged 26, killed at John Prescott's garrison; Henry
Farrar; Richard Wheeler; a man mentioned by Mrs. Rowlandson,
but not named. *Captives:* Two of John Ball's family, names un-
known.

Others killed or taken captive (5)
John Kettle and two sons, escaped; a soldier from Watertown was
killed near Prescott's mill a few days later; John Roper was slain on
the day the town was finally abandoned.

This list accounts for *forty-eight;* if fifty-five is the correct number, it will be seen that several are still missing.

pany of sheep torn by wolves. All of them stripped naked by a company of hell-hounds, roaring, singing, ranting and insulting, as if they would have torn our very hearts out; yet the Lord by his almighty power preserved a number of us from death, for there were twenty-four of us taken alive and carried captive.

I had often before this said, that if the Indians should come, I should choose rather to be killed by them, than taken alive; but when it came to the trial, my mind changed; their glittering weapons so daunted my spirit, that I chose rather to go along with those (as I may say) ravenous bears, than that moment to end my days. And that I may the better declare what happened to me during that grievous captivity, I shall particularly speak of the several Removes we had up and down the wilderness.

The First Remove [8]

Now away we must go with those barbarous creatures, with our bodies wounded and bleeding, and our hearts no less than our bodies. About a mile we went that night, up upon a hill within sight of the town, [9]

[8] Thursday night, February 10, 1675/6.

[9] This camp was upon George Hill, the highest elevation in Lancaster, so named by the first planters probably because George Adams as early as 1645 had his home lot of twenty acres upon it adjoining the site of Symonds' and King's trucking-house. Upon the summit is a huge granite boulder, rent in twain and half buried, which time-hallowed tradition has honored as the resting-place of the captive the night after the sack of the town. The "vacant house" was that originally occupied by John Prescott, built on the trucking-house site.

where they intended to lodge. There was hard by a vacant house (deserted by the English before, for fear of the Indians). I asked them whether I might not lodge in the house that night, to which they made answer, what, will you love Englishmen still? This was the dolefulest night that ever my eyes saw. Oh the roaring and singing and dancing and yelling of those black creatures in the night, which made the place[10] a lively resemblance of hell; and as miserable was the waste that was there made, of horses, cattle, sheep, swine, calves, lambs, roasting pigs, and fowl, (which they had plundered in the town,) some roasting, some lying and burning, and some boiling, to feed our merciless enemies, who were joyful enough, though we were disconsolate. To add to the dolefulness of the former day, and the dismalness of the present night, my thoughts ran upon my losses and sad bereaved condition. All was gone, my husband gone, (at least separated from me, he being in the Bay;[11] and to add to my grief, the Indians told me they would kill him as he came homeward;) my children gone, my relations and friends gone, our house and home and all our comforts within door and without, all was gone, except my life, and I knew not but the next moment that might go too. There remained nothing to me but one poor wounded babe,

[10] Second edition prints "peace," but "place" seems to be meant.

[11] The Reverend Mr. Rowlandson had gone to Boston, i.e., "to the Bay," to persuade the Governor to send soldiers to Lancaster to guard them against an Indian attack. But the Indians arrived before he succeeded in his enterprise.

and it seemed at present worse than death, that it was in such a pitiful condition, bespeaking compassion, and I had no refreshing for it, nor suitable things to revive it. Little do many think what is the savageness and brutishness of this barbarous enemy, even those that seem to profess more than others among them, when the English have fallen into their hands.

Those seven that were killed at Lancaster the summer before upon a Sabbath day,[12] and the one that was afterwards killed upon a week day, were slain and mangled in a barbarous manner, by One-eyed John, and Marlborough "Praying Indians," which Captain Moseley brought to Boston, as the Indians told me.

The Second Remove [13]

But now, the next morning, I must turn my back upon the town, and travel with them into the vast

[12] These victims of August 22, 1675, were: George Bennett, Jacob Farrar, Jr., Joseph Wheeler, William Flagg, and Mordecai McLoud with his wife Lydia (Lewis) and two young children. Flagg was a soldier belonging to Watertown. The leader of the blood-thirsty horde guilty of these murders was Monoco, *alias* One-eyed John, a Nashaway, one of the most cunning and merciless of the Indian chieftains known to New England history. He was the prominent figure in the tragedies at Brookfield, Medfield, and Groton, and made the boast that he would carry devastation town by town to the Bay. He was finally hung at Boston, September 26, 1676. The Christian or "praying" Indians were not guilty. Mrs. Rowlandson was misinformed.

[13] Friday, February 11. The second night's encampment was upon the Indian trail, and probably in the western part of Princeton. This trail ran a little south of Mount Wachusett to the Indian villages on the Menameset (now Ware) River.

and desolate wilderness, I knew not whither. It is
not my tongue nor pen can express the sorrows of my
heart, and bitterness of my spirit, that I had at this
departure: but God was with me in a wonderful manner, carrying me along, and bearing up my spirit,
that it did not quite fail. One of the Indians carried
my poor wounded babe upon a horse; it went moan-
ing all along, I shall die, I shall die. I went on foot
after it, with sorrow that cannot be expressed. At
length I took it off the horse and carried it in my arms
till my strength failed, and I fell down with it. Then
they set me upon a horse with my wounded child in
my lap, and there being no furniture upon the horse's
back, as we went down a steep hill, we both fell over
the horse's head at which they like inhuman creatures
laughed, and rejoiced to see it, though I thought we
should there have ended our days, overcome with so
many difficulties. But the Lord renewed my strength
still, and carried me along that I might see more of
his power; yea, so much that I could never have
thought of, had I not experienced it.

After this it quickly began to snow and when night
came on they stopped. And now I must sit down in
the snow before a little fire, and a few boughs behind
me, with my sick child in my lap, and calling much
for water, being now (through the wound) fallen into
a violent fever. My own wound also growing so stiff
that I could scarce sit down or rise up; yet so it must
be that I must sit all this cold winter night upon the
cold snowy ground, with my sick child in my arms,

looking that every hour would be the last of its life, and having no Christian friend near me, either to comfort or help me. Oh, I may see the wonderful power of God, that my spirit did not utterly sink under my afflictions; still the Lord upheld me with his gracious and merciful spirit, and we were both alive to see the light of the next morning.

The Third Remove [14]

The morning being come, they prepared to go on their way. One of the Indians got up on a horse and they set me up behind him with my poor sick babe in my lap. A very wearisome and tedious day I had of it; what with my own wound, and my child being so exceedingly sick, and in a lamentable condition with her wound. It may be easily judged what a poor feeble condition we were in, there being not the least crumb of refreshment that came within either of our mouths from Wednesday night to Saturday night, except only a little cold water. This day in the afternoon, about an hour by sun, we came to the place where they intended, viz., an Indian town called Wenimesset, northward of Quabaug.[15] When we were come, oh the number of pagans (our merciless enemies) that there came about me! I might say as David, Psal. xxvii. 13. *I had fainted, unless I had be-*

[14] Saturday, February 12, to Sunday, February 27.

[15] Wenimessett or Meminimisset was a swamp stronghold of the Quabaug Indians in the extreme northern angle of the town of New Braintree.

lieved, &c. The next day was the Sabbath. I then remembered how careless I had been of God's holy
time; how many Sabbaths I had lost and misspent,
and how evilly I had walked in God's sight; which
lay so closely upon my spirit, that it was easy for me
to see how righteous it was with God to cut off the
thread of my life, and cast me out of his presence for-
ever. Yet the Lord still showed mercy to me, and upheld me; and as he wounded me with one hand, so he
healed me with the other. This day there came to me
one Robert Pepper [16] (a man belonging to Roxbury)
who was taken in Captain Beers' fight, and had now
been a considerable time with the Indians, and up
with them almost as far as Albany to see King Philip,
as he told me, and was now very lately come into
these parts.[17] Hearing, I say, that I was in this Indian town, he obtained leave to come and see me. He

[16] Captain Richard Beers, of Watertown, and thirty-six men,
while on their way to reënforce the Northfield garrison, were way-
laid by a party of over one hundred warriors, September 3, 1675,
two miles south of their destination, when the leader and nineteen
soldiers were slain. Pepper was captured; the rest escaped.

[17] This captive's statement respecting Philip is very important,
and seems to have been overlooked by many historians. It must
be accepted when associated with other contemporary records as a
complete confutation of the tradition that Philip led the assault
upon Lancaster. Philip could not have been within one hundred
miles of Lancaster on the day of the assault. Muttaump, *alias*
Maliompe, sachem of the Quabaugs, was the senior chieftain
present, and Sagamore Sam and Monoco, *alias* One-eyed John, of
the Nashaways, Matoonas of the Nipmucks, and Quanopin of the
Narragansets, were his lieutenants. They led in all about four
hundred warriors.

told me he himself was wounded in the leg at Captain Beers' fight and was not able [for] some time to go, but as they carried him, and as he took oak leaves and laid to his wound, and through the blessing of God he was able to travel again. Then I took oak leaves and laid to my side, and with the blessing of God it cured me also; yet before the cure was wrought, I may say, as it is in Psal. xxxviii. 5, 6. *My wounds stink and are corrupt, I am troubled, I am bowed down greatly, I go mourning all the day long.* I sat much alone with my poor wounded child in my lap, which moaned night and day, having nothing to revive the body, or cheer the spirits of her; but instead of that, sometimes one Indian would come and tell me one hour, that your master will knock your child in the head, and then a second, and then a third, your master will quickly knock your child in the head.

This was all the comfort I had from them, miserable comforters are ye all, as he said. Thus nine days I sat upon my knees with my babe upon my lap, till my flesh was raw again. My child being even ready to depart this sorrowful world, they bade me carry it out to another wigwam, (I suppose because they would not be troubled with such spectacles,) whither I went with a very heavy heart, and down I sat with the picture of death in my lap. About two hours in the night my sweet babe, like a lamb, departed this life, on February 18, 1675, it being about six years and five months old. It was about nine days from the first wounding in this miserable condition, without

any refreshing of one nature or another, except a little
cold water. I cannot but take notice, how at another
time I could not bear to be in the room where any
dead person was, but now the case is changed; I
must, and can lie down by my dead babe, side by
side, all the night after. I have thought since of the
wonderful goodness of God to me, in preserving me in
the use of my reason and sense in that distressed time,
that I did not use wicked and violent means to end
my own miserable life. In the morning when they
understood that my child was dead, they sent for me
home to my master's wigwam, (by my master in this
writing must be understood Quanopin, who was a
Sagamore, and married King Philip's wife's sister;
not that he first took me, but I was sold to him by
another Narraganset Indian, who took me when first
I came out of the garrison.) I went to take up my
dead child in my arms to carry it with me, but they
bid me let it alone: there was no resisting, but go I
must and leave it. When I had been [awhile] at my
master's wigwam, I took the first opportunity I could
get to go look after my dead child. When I came I
asked them what they had done with it. Then they
told me it was upon the hill, — then they went and
showed me where it was, where I saw the ground was
newly digged, and there they told me they had buried
it. There I left that child in the wilderness, and must
commit it, and myself also, in this wilderness condition to him who is above all. God having taken away
this dear child, I went to see my daughter Mary, who

was at this same Indian town at a wigwam not very far off, though we had little liberty or opportunity to see one another. She was about ten years old, and taken from the door at first by a Praying Indian and afterward sold for a gun. When I came in sight she would fall a-weeping, at which they were provoked, and would not let me come near her, but bade me be gone, which was a heart-cutting word to me. I had one child dead, another in the wilderness I knew not where, the third they would not let me come near to. *Me* (as he said) *have ye bereaved of my children, Joseph is not, and Simon is not, and ye will take Benjamin also: all these things are against me.* I could not sit still in this condition, but kept walking from one place to another. And as I was going along, my heart was even overwhelmed with the thoughts of my condition, and that I should have children, and a nation which I knew not ruled over them. Whereupon I earnestly entreated the Lord that he would consider my low estate and show me a token for good, and if it were his blessed will, some sign and hope for some relief.

And indeed quickly the Lord answered, in some measure, my poor prayers; for as I was going up and down mourning and lamenting my condition, my son came to me and asked me how I did. I had not seen him before since the destruction of the town, and I knew not where he was, till I was informed by himself, that he was amongst a smaller parcel of Indians, whose place was about six miles off. With tears in his

eyes he asked me whether his sister Sarah was dead,
and told me he had seen his sister Mary, and prayed
me that I would not be troubled in reference to himself. The occasion of his coming to see me at this time
was this: There was, as I said, about six miles from us,
a small plantation of Indians, where it seems he had
been during his captivity, and at this time there were
some forces of the Indians gathered out of our company, and some also from them, (amongst whom was
my son's master) to go to the assault and burn Medfield.[18] In this time of the absence of his master, his
dame brought him to see me. I took this to be some
gracious answer to my earnest and unfeigned desire.

The next day, viz. to this, the Indians returned
from Medfield; (all the company, for those that be-
longed to the other small company came through the
town that now we were at.) But before they came to
us, oh the outrageous roaring and whooping that there
was! They began their din about a mile before they
came to us. By their noise and whooping, they signi-
fied how many they had destroyed, (which was at that
time twenty-three.) Those that were with us at home
were gathered together as soon as they heard the
whooping, and every time that the other went over
their number, these at home gave a shout, that the
very earth rang again. And thus they continued till
those that had been upon the expedition were come

[18] This town, though less than twenty miles from Boston, was
attacked February 21, when fifty houses were burned and eighteen
persons slain.

up to the Sagamore's wigwam; and then, oh the hideous insulting and triumphing that there was over some Englishmen's scalps that they had taken (as their manner is) and brought with them. I cannot but take notice of the wonderful mercy of God to me in those afflictions, in sending me a Bible. One of the Indians that came from Medfield fight had brought some plunder, came to me, and asked me if I would have a Bible. He had got one in his basket. I was glad of it and asked him whether he thought the Indians would let me read [it]. He answered, yes. So I took the Bible and in that melancholy time it came into my mind to read first the 28th chapter of Deuteronomy, which I did. And when I had read it my dark heart wrought on this manner: That there was no mercy for me, that the blessings were gone and the curses came in their room, and that I had lost my opportunity. But the Lord helped me still to go on reading till I came to chapter 30, the seven first verses, where I found there was mercy promised again if we would return to him by repentence; and though we were scattered from one end of the earth to the other, yet the Lord would gather us together, and turn all those curses upon our enemies. I do not desire to live to forget this scripture, and what comfort it was to me.

Now the Indians began to talk of removing from this place, some one way, and some another. There were now besides myself nine English captives in this place, (all of them children, except one woman.) I got an opportunity to go and take my leave of them, they being to go one way and I another. I asked them whether they were earnest with God for deliverance. They told me they did as they were able and it was some comfort to me that the Lord stirred up children to look to him. The woman, viz. Goodwife Joslin, told me she should never see me again and that she could find in her heart to run away. I wished her not to run away by any means, for we were near thirty miles from any English town and she very big with child, and had but one week to reckon; and another child in her arms, two years old, and bad rivers there were to go over, and we were feeble with our poor and coarse entertainment. I had my Bible with me: I pulled it out and asked her whether she would read. We opened the Bible and lighted on Psal. xxvii., in which Psalm we especially took notice of that verse, viz., *Wait on the Lord, be of good courage, and he shall strengthen thine heart; wait I say on the Lord.*

THE FOURTH REMOVE [19]

And now I must part with that little company I had. Here I parted from my daughter Mary, (whom I never saw again till I saw her in Dorchester, returned from captivity,) and from four little cousins and neighbors, some of whom I never saw afterward:

[19] Monday, February 28, to Friday, March 3. This camp was probably within the limits of Petersham, about half-way between the Ware and Miller's Rivers, and near the Indian village of Nichewaug.

the Lord only knows the end of them. Amongst them also was that poor woman before mentioned, who came to a sad end as some of the company told me in my travel; she having much grief upon her spirit, about her miserable condition, being so near her time, she would be often asking the Indians to let her go home. They not being willing to do that, and yet vexed with her importunity, gathered a great company about her and stripped her naked and set her in the midst of them. And when they had sung and danced about her (in their hellish manner) as long as they pleased, they knocked her on the head and the child in her arms with her. When they had done that, they made a fire and put them both into it and told the other children that were there with them that if they attempted to go home, they would serve them in like manner. The children said she did not shed one tear but prayed all the while. But to return to my own journey: we travelled about half a day or little more, and came to a desolate place in the wilderness where there were no wigwams or inhabitants before. We came about the middle of the afternoon to this place, cold and wet, and snowy, and hungry, and weary, and no refreshing for man but the cold ground to sit on and our poor Indian cheer.

Heart-aching thoughts here I had about my poor children who were scattered up and down among the wild beasts of the forest. My head was light and dizzy, (either through hunger or hard lodging, or trouble, or all together,) my knees feeble, my body raw by sitting double night and day, that I cannot express to man the affliction that lay upon my spirit. But the Lord helped me at that time to express it to himself. I opened my Bible to read, and the Lord brought that precious scripture to me: Jeremiah xxxi. 16. *Thus saith the Lord, refrain thy voice from weeping, and thine eyes from tears, for thy work shall be rewarded, and they shall come again from the land of the enemy.* This was a sweet cordial to me when I was ready to faint. Many and many a time have I sat down and wept sweetly over this scripture. At this place we continued about four days.

THE FIFTH REMOVE [20]

The occasion (as I thought) of their removing at this time, was the English army, it being near and following them, for they went, as if they had gone for their lives, for some considerable way and then they made a stop and chose some of their stoutest men and sent them back to hold the English army in play whilst the rest escaped. And then, like Jehu, they marched on furiously with their old and their young. Some carried their old decrepit mothers, some carried

[20] Friday, March 3, to March 5. The crossing over the Baquag, or Miller's, River was in Orange, near the Athol line. The "English army" in pursuit was a troop of mounted men and three infantry companies from the Bay towns, with a similar force from Connecticut, all under the command of Major Thomas Savage. They reached Quabaug (North Brookfield) March 2 and, had they not been detained by Indian wiles, the cavalry should have overtaken the retreating mob of savages before they effected their crossing of the swollen stream.

one, and some another. Four of them carried a great
Indian upon a bier; but going through a thick wood
with him they were hindered and could make no
haste; whereupon they took him on their backs, and
carried him, one at a time, till they came to Baquag
River. Upon a Friday, a little after noon we came to
this river. When all the company was come up, and
were gathered together, I thought to count the number of them but they were so many, and being somewhat in motion, it was beyond my skill. In this travel,
because of my wound, I was somewhat favored in
my load: I carried only my knitting work and two
quarts of parched meal. Being very faint I asked my
mistress to give me one spoonful of the meal but she
would not give me a taste. They quickly fell to cut-
ting dry trees to make rafts to carry them over the
river, and soon my turn came to go over. By the advantage of some brush, which they had laid upon the
raft to sit upon, I did not wet my foot (while many of
themselves at the other end were mid-leg deep) which
cannot but be acknowledged as a favor of God to my
weakened body, it being a very cold time. I was not
before acquainted with such kind of doings or dan-
gers. *When thou passest through the waters, I will be
with thee, and through the rivers, they shall not overflow
thee.* Isaiah xliii. 2. A certain number of us got over
the river that night but it was the night after the
Sabbath before all the company was got over. On the
Saturday they boiled an old horse's leg (which they
had got) and so we drank of the broth as soon as they

thought it was ready, and when it was almost gone they filled it up again.

The first week of my being among them I hardly ate anything; the second week I found my stomach grow very faint for want of something, and yet it was very hard to get down their filthy trash. But the third week, though I could think how formerly my stomach would turn against this or that, and I could starve and die before I could eat such things, yet they were very sweet and savory to my taste. I was at this time knitting a pair of white cotton stockings for my mistress, and had not yet wrought upon the Sabbath day. When the Sabbath came they bade me go to work. I told them it was the Sabbath day and desired them to let me rest, and told them I would do as much more tomorrow: to which they answered, they would break my face. And here I cannot but take notice of the strange providence of God in preserving the heathen: they were many hundreds, old and young, some sick, and some lame; many had papooses on their backs; the greatest number at this time with us were squaws, and they travelled with all they had, bag and baggage, and yet they got over this river aforesaid. And on Monday they set their wigwams on fire, and away they went. On that very day came the English army after them to this river, and saw the smoke of their wigwams, and yet this river put a stop to them. God did not give them courage or activity to go over after us. We were not ready for so great a mercy as victory and deliverance; if we had been God would have found out a way for the English to have passed this river, as well as for the Indians with their squaws and children and all their luggage. *Oh that my people had hearkened to me, and Israel had walked in my ways, I should soon have subdued their enemies, and turned my hand against their adversaries.* Psalm lxxxi. 13, 14.

The Sixth Remove [21]

On Monday (as I said) they set their wigwams on fire, and went away. It was a cold morning and before us there was a great brook with ice on it; some waded through it up to the knees and higher, but others went until they came to a beaver dam, and I amongst them, where through the good providence of God, I did not wet my foot. I went along that day mourning and lamenting, leaving farther my own country, and travelling into the vast and howling wilderness, and I understood something of Lot's wife's temptation, when she looked back. We came that day to a great swamp by the side of which we took up our lodging that night. When I came to the brow of the hill that looked towards the swamp I thought we had been come to a great Indian town (though there were none but our own company). The Indians were as thick as trees. It seemed as if there had been a thousand hatchets going at once. If one looked be-

[21] Monday, March 6. This night's bivouac was beside the great Northfield Swamp on the trail between Nichewaug (Petersham) and Squakeag (Northfield).

fore one there was nothing but Indians, and behind one, nothing but Indians, and so on either hand, I myself in the midst and no Christian soul near me, and yet how hath the Lord preserved me in safety! Oh the experience that I have had of the goodness of God, to me and mine!

THE SEVENTH REMOVE [22]

After a restless and hungry night there, we had a wearisome time of it the next day. The swamp, by which we lay, was as it were a deep dungeon, and an exceeding high and steep hill before it. Before I got to the top of the hill I thought my heart and legs and all would have broken and failed me. What through faintness and soreness of body it was a grievous day of travel to me. As we went along I saw a place where English cattle had been: that was comfort to me, such as it was. Quickly after that we came to an English path which so took with me that I thought I could have freely lain down and died. That day, a little after noon, we came to Squakeag [23] where the Indians quickly spread themselves over the deserted English fields, gleaning what they could find, — some picked up ears of wheat that were crickled down, some found ears of Indian corn, some found groundnuts, and others sheaves of wheat that were frozen together in the shock, and went to threshing of them out. Myself

[22] Tuesday, March 7. This night's camp was at Squakeag, near Beers' Plain in Northfield.

[23] Northfield, Massachusetts.

got two ears of Indian corn, and whilst I did but turn my back, one of them was stolen from me, which much troubled me. There came an Indian to them at that time with a basket of horse-liver. I asked him to give me a piece. What, says he, can you eat horse-liver? I told him I would try if he would give me a piece, which he did, and I laid it on the coals to roast; but before it was half ready, they got half of it away from me, so that I was fain to take the rest and eat it as it was, with the blood about my mouth, and yet a savory bit it was to me: for the hungry soul every bitter thing is sweet. A solemn sight methought it was to see the fields of wheat and Indian corn forsaken and spoiled, and the remainders of them to be food for our merciless enemies. That night we had a mess of wheat for our supper.

The Eighth Remove [24]

On the morrow morning we must go over the river, i.e. Connecticut, to meet with King Philip. Two canoes full they had carried over: the next turn myself was to go, but as my foot was upon the canoe to step in there was a sudden out-cry among them and I must step back. And instead of going over the river, I must go four or five miles up the river farther northward. Some of the Indians ran one way, and some another. The cause of this rout was, as I thought, their espying some English scouts, who were there-

[24] Wednesday, March 8. This encampment, on the west side of the Connecticut River, was at Coasset in South Vernon, Vermont.

about. In this travel up the river, about noon the
company made a stop and sat down; some to eat, and
others to rest them. As I sat amongst them musing of
things past my son Joseph unexpectedly came to me.
We asked of each others welfare, bemoaning our doleful condition, and the change that had come upon us.
We had husband, and father, and children, and sisters,
and friends, and relations, and house, and home, and
many comforts of this life; but now we may say, as
Job: *Naked came I out of my mother's womb, and naked
shall I return. The Lord gave, and the Lord hath taken
away; blessed be the name of the Lord.* I asked him
whether he would read: he told me he earnestly desired it. I gave him my Bible and he lighted upon
that comfortable scripture, Psalm cxviii. 17, 18. *I
shall not die, but live, and declare the works of the Lord:
The Lord hath chastened me sore, yet he hath not given
me over to death.* Look here, mother, (says he,) did
you read this? And here I may take occasion to mention one principal ground of my setting forth these
lines: even as the Psalmist says, To declare the works
of the Lord, and his wonderful power in carrying us
along, preserving us in the wilderness, while under
the enemies hand, and returning of us in safety again.
And his goodness in bringing to my hand so many
comfortable and suitable scriptures in my distress.

But to return: We travelled on till night, and in the
morning we must go over the river to Philip's crew.
When I was in the canoe I could not but be amazed at
the numerous crew of pagans that were on the bank

on the other side. When I came ashore they gathered
all about me, I sitting alone in the midst. I observed
they asked one another questions, and laughed, and
rejoiced over their gains and victories. Then my heart
began to fail and I fell a-weeping, which was the first
time to my remembrance that I wept before them. Al-
though I had met with so much affliction and my
heart was many times ready to break, yet could I not
shed one tear in their sight, but rather had been all
this while in a maze, and like one astonished. But
now I may say as Psalm cxxxvii. 1. *By the rivers of
Babylon, there we sat down, yea, we wept when we remembered Zion.* There one of them asked me why I
wept. I could hardly tell what to say, yet I answered,
they would kill me. No, said he, none will hurt you.
Then came one of them and gave me two spoonfuls
of meal to comfort me and another gave me half a
pint of peas, which was worth more than many
bushels at another time. Then I went to see King
Philip.[25] He bade me come in and sit down, and asked
me whether I would smoke it, (a usual compliment
now-a-days amongst saints and sinners) but this no
way suited me. For though I had formerly used to-

[25] This was evidently her first meeting with Philip. He had only
recently reached the Connecticut Valley, returning from his winter
quarters on the Hudson, whither he had gone with (as Governor
Andros estimated) about a thousand warriors, for the purpose of
buying powder and shot of the Dutch, and in the hope of enticing
the Mohawks or Canadian Indians into an alliance against the
Massachusetts colonists. At Coasset there congregated all the
hostile tribes, an assemblage numbering perhaps two thousand
fighting men.

bacco, yet I had left it ever since I was first taken. It seems to be a bait the devil lays to make men lose their precious time. I remember with shame, how formerly, when I had taken two or three pipes I was ready for another, such a bewitching thing it is. But I thank God he has now given me power over it. Surely there are many who may be better employed than to lie sucking a stinking tobacco-pipe.

Now the Indians gather their forces to go against Northampton. Over night one went about yelling and hooting to give notice of the design. Whereupon they fell to boiling of ground-nuts and parching of corn (as many as had it) for their provision; and in the morning away they went. During my abode in this place Philip spake to me to make a shirt for his boy, which I did, for which he gave me a shilling. I offered the money to my master but he bade me keep it, and with it I bought a piece of horse flesh. Afterwards he asked me to make a cap for his boy, for which he invited me to dinner. I went, and he gave me a pancake, about as big as two fingers. It was made of parched wheat, beaten, and fried in bear's grease, but I thought I had never tasted pleasanter meat in my life. There was a squaw who spake to me to make a shirt for her sannup, for which she gave me a piece of bear. Another asked me to knit a pair of stockings for which she gave me a quart of peas. I boiled my peas and bear together, and invited my master and mistress to dinner, but the proud gossip, because I served them both in one dish, would eat nothing, except one bit that he gave her upon the point of his knife.

Hearing that my son was come to this place, I went to see him and found him lying flat upon the ground. I asked him how he could sleep so. He answered me that he was not asleep but at prayer, and lay so that they might not observe what he was doing. I pray God he may remember these things now he is returned in safety. At this place (the sun now getting higher) what with the beams and heat of the sun and the smoke of the wigwams, I thought I should have been blind. I could scarce discern one wigwam from another. There was one Mary Thurston of Medfield who, seeing how it was with me, lent me a hat to wear. But as soon as I was gone the squaw that owned that Mary Thurston came running after me and got it away again. Here was the squaw that gave me one spoonful of meal. I put it in my pocket to keep it safe, yet notwithstanding, somebody stole it but put five Indian corns in the room of it, which corns were the greatest provisions I had in my travel for one day.

The Indians returning from Northampton [26] brought with them some horses and sheep and others things which they had taken. I desired them that they would carry me to Albany upon one of those horses and sell me for powder; for so they sometimes discoursed. I was utterly hopeless of getting home on

[26] The attack here mentioned was on March 14, and the town having been recently palisaded the enemy was repulsed, six of the inhabitants being slain and three or four houses burned.

foot, the way that I came. I could hardly bear to think of the many weary steps I had taken to come to this place.

THE NINTH REMOVE [27]

But instead of going either to Albany or homeward, we must go five miles up the river and then go over it. Here we abode a while. Here lived a sorry Indian who spake to me to make him a shirt: when I had done it he would pay me nothing. But he, living by the river side where I often went to fetch water, I would often be putting of him in mind and calling for my pay. At last he told me if I would make another shirt for a papoose not yet born he would give me a knife, which he did when I had done it. I carried the knife in, and my master asked me to give it him, and I was not a little glad that I had anything that they would accept of and be pleased with. When we were at this place, my master's maid came home. She had been gone three weeks into the Narraganset country to fetch corn, where they had stored up some in the ground. She brought home about a peck and a half of corn. This was about the time that their great captain, Naananto,[28] was killed in the Narraganset country.

[27] This encampment was in the Ashuelot Valley, New Hampshire.

[28] The King of the Narragansets, better known as Canonchet, the son of Miantonimo, was not captured until April 2. He was feared by the English hardly less than Philip; and with better reason, for he was the brains of the savage confederation, the influence and prowess of Philip being much overestimated in history. Canonchet with a party of about seventy-five, including thirty

My son being now about a mile from me, I asked liberty to go and see him. They bade me go and away I went, but quickly lost myself travelling over hills and through swamps, and could not find the way to him. And I cannot but admire at the wonderful power and goodness of God to me, in that, though I was gone from home, and met with all sorts of Indians, and those I had no knowledge of, and there being no Christian soul near me, yet not one of them offered the least imaginable miscarriage to me. I turned homeward again and met with my master. He showed me the way to my son. When I came to him I found him not well and withal he had a boil on his side which much troubled him. We bemoaned one another there awhile, as the Lord helped us, and then I returned again. When I returned I found myself as unsatisfied as I was before. I went up and down mourning and lamenting, and my spirit was ready to sink with the thoughts of my poor children: my son was ill and I could not but think of his mournful looks, and no Christian friend was near him to do any office of love for him either for soul or body. And my poor girl, I knew not where she was, not whether she was sick, or well, or alive, or dead. I repaired under these

warriors, visited the Narraganset country to secure a store of feed corn from secret granaries near Seekonk belonging to his people. The corn was obtained and some of it reached the Squakeag encampment, but Canonchet with a small escort was surprised and captured by a scouting party under Captain George Denison. Canonchet was shot the next day at Stonington, and from that time the alliance of the hostile tribes began to lose coherence.

thoughts to my Bible (my great comfort in that time) and that scripture came to my hand, *Cast thy burden upon the Lord, and he shall sustain thee.* Psalm lv. 22.

But I was fain to go and look after something to satisfy my hunger, and going among the wigwams I went into one and there found a squaw who showed herself very kind to me and gave me a piece of bear. I put it into my pocket and came home but could not find an opportunity to boil it, for fear they would get it from me, and there it lay all day and night in my stinking pocket. In the morning I went to the same squaw who had a kettle of ground-nuts boiling. I asked her to let me boil my piece of bear in her kettle, which she did, and gave me some ground-nuts to eat with it, and I cannot but think how pleasant it was to me. I have sometimes seen bear baked very handsomely among the English, and some liked it; but the thought that it was bear made me tremble. But now that was savory to me that one would think was enough to turn the stomach of a brute creature.

One bitter cold day I could find no room to sit down before the fire. I went out and could not tell what to do, but I went into another wigwam where they were also sitting round the fire. But the squaw laid a skin for me and bid me sit down and gave me some ground-nuts and bade me come again; and told me they would buy me if they were able, and yet these were strangers to me that I never saw before.

The Tenth Remove [29]

That day a small part of the company removed about three-quarters of a mile intending further the next day. When they came to the place where they intended to lodge and had pitched their wigwams, being hungry I went again back to the place we were before at, to get something to eat, being encouraged by the squaw's kindness, who bade me come again. When I was there there came an Indian to look after me, who when he had found me, kicked me all along. I went home and found venison roasting that night but they would not give me a bit of it. Sometimes I met with favor and sometimes with nothing but frowns.

The Eleventh Remove [30]

The next day in the morning they took their travel intending a day's journey up the river. I took my load at my back and quickly we came to wade over the river, and passed some tiresome and wearisome hills. One hill was so steep that I was fain to creep up upon my knees and to hold by the twigs and bushes to keep myself from falling back. My head also was so light that I usually reeled as I went, but I hope all

[29] Still in Ashuelot Valley.

[30] This remove took the captive to the northernmost point reached by her. The encampment was near the Connecticut River in Chesterfield, New Hampshire, or perhaps in Westmoreland. A "day's journey" for an Indian band including women and children, travelling single file through the wilderness with all their belongings, was rarely much over ten miles, as their itinerary proves.

these wearisome steps that I have taken are but a forewarning to me of the heavenly rest. *I know, O Lord, that thy judgments are right, and that thou in faithfulness hast afflicted me.* Psalm cxix. 75.

THE TWELFTH REMOVE [31]

It was upon a Sabbath-day-morning that they prepared for their travel. This morning I asked my master whether he would sell me to my husband. He answered me "*Nuк*," which did much rejoice my spirit. My mistress, before she went, was gone to the burial of a papoose, and returning she found me sitting and reading in my Bible. She snatched it hastily out of my hand and threw it out of doors. I ran out and catched it up and put it in my pocket and never let her see it afterwards. Then they packed up their things to be gone and gave me my load. I complained it was too heavy, whereupon she gave me a slap in the face, and bade me go. I lifted up my heart to God, hoping the redemption was not far off, and the rather because their insolency grew worse and worse.

But the thoughts of my going homeward (for so we bent our course) much cheered my spirit and made my burden seem light, and almost nothing at all. But (to my amazement and great perplexity) the scale was soon turned; for when we had gone a little way, on a sudden my mistress gives out, she would go no further, but turn back again, and said I must go

[31] Sunday, April 9. The camp was in the same neighborhood as the last.

back again with her. And she called her sannup, and
would have had him gone back also, but he would not,
and said he would go on and come back to us again in
three days. My spirit was upon this, I confess, very
impatient and almost outrageous. I thought I could
as well have died as went back. I cannot declare the
trouble that I was in about it, but yet back again I
must go. As soon as I had an opportunity, I took my
Bible to read, and that quieting scripture came to my
hand, Psalm xlvi. 10, *Be still and know that I am God,*
which stilled my spirit for the present; but a sore time
of trial I concluded I had to go through. My master
being gone, who seemed to me the best friend that I
had of an Indian, both in cold and hunger; and quickly
so it proved. Down I sat with my heart as full as it
could hold and yet so hungry that I could not sit
neither. But going out to see what I could find, and
walking among the trees, I found six acorns and two
chestnuts, which were some refreshment to me. Towards night I gathered me some sticks for my own
comfort that I might not lie down a-cold, but when
we came to lie down they bade me go out and lie
some where else for they had company, (they said)
come in more than their own. I told them I could not
tell where to go; they bade me go look. I told them if
I went to another wigwam they would be angry and
send me home again. Then one of the company drew
his sword and told me he would run me through if I
did not go presently. Then was I fain to stoop to this
rude fellow and go out into the night I knew not

whither. Mine eyes have seen that fellow afterwards
walking up and down Boston under the appearance
of a friendly Indian, and several others of the like cut.
I went to one wigwam and they told me they had no
room. Then I went to another and they told me the
same. At last an old Indian bade me come to him,
and his squaw gave me some ground-nuts. She gave
me also something to lay under my head, and a good
fire we had, and through the good providence of God I
had a comfortable lodging that night. In the morning
another Indian bade me come at night and he would
give me six ground-nuts, which I did. We were at this
place and time about two miles from Connecticut
river. We went in the morning to gather ground-nuts,
to the river, and went back again that night. I went
with a good load at my back (for they, when they
went, though but a little way, would carry all their
trumpery with them.) I told them the skin was off
my back but I had no other comforting answer from
them than this, that it would be no matter if my head
were off too.

THE THIRTEENTH REMOVE [32]

Instead of going toward the Bay (which was what
I desired) I must go with them five or six miles down
the river into a mighty thicket of brush where we
abode almost a fortnight. Here one asked me to make
a shirt for her papoose, for which she gave me a mess

[32] This fortnight's encampment was probably in the south part
of Hinsdale, New Hampshire, near the river.

of broth, which was thickened with meal made of the bark of a tree, and to make it better she put into it about a handful of peas and a few roasted ground-nuts. I had not seen my son for a pretty while and here was an Indian of whom I made inquiry after him and asked him when he saw him. He answered me that such a time his master roasted him and that himself did eat a piece of him as big as his two fingers, and that he was very good meat. But the Lord upheld my spirit under this discouragement, and I considered their horrible addictedness to lying, and that there is not one of them that makes the least conscience of speaking the truth. In this place on a cold night as I lay by the fire I removed a stick that kept the heat from me: a squaw moved it down again, at which I looked up and she threw a handful of ashes in mine eyes. I thought I should have been quite blinded and have never seen more. But lying down, the water ran out of my eyes and carried the dirt with it [so] that by the morning I recovered my sight again. Yet upon this, and the like occasions, I hope it is not too much to say with Job, *Have pity upon me, have pity upon me, O ye my friends, for the hand of the Lord has touched me.* And here I cannot but remember how many times, sitting in their wigwams and musing on things past, I should suddenly leap up and run out as if I had been at home, forgetting where I was and what my condition was. But when I was without and saw nothing but wilderness and woods and a company of barbarous heathens, my mind quickly returned to me, which made me think of that spoken concerning Samson, who said, *I will go out and shake myself as at other times, but he wist not that the Lord was departed from him.*

About this time I began to think that all my hopes of restoration would come to nothing. I thought of the English army and hoped for their coming and being taken by them, but that failed. I hope to be carried to Albany, as the Indians had discoursed before, but that failed also. I thought of being sold to my husband, as my master spake, but instead of that my master himself was gone and I left behind so that my spirit was now quite ready to sink. I asked them to let me go out and pick up some sticks that I might get alone, and pour out my heart unto the Lord. Then also I took my Bible to read, but I found no comfort here neither, which many times I was wont to find, so easy a thing is it with God to dry up the streams of scripture comfort from us. Yet I can say that in all my sorrows and afflictions God did not leave me to have my impatience work towards himself, as if his ways were unrighteous. But I knew that he laid upon me less than I deserved. Afterwards, before this doleful time ended with me, I was turning the leaves of my Bible and the Lord brought to me some scriptures which did a little revive me, as that, Isaiah lv. 8, *For my thoughts are not your thoughts, neither are your ways my ways saith the Lord.* And also, that, Psalm xxxvii. 5, *Commit thy ways unto the Lord, trust also in him, and he shall bring it to pass.*

About this time they came yelping from Hadley,[33] where they had killed three Englishmen, and brought one captive with them, viz., Thomas Read. They all gathered about the poor man asking him many questions. I desired also to go and see him; and when I came he was weeping bitterly supposing they would quickly kill him. Whereupon I asked one of them whether they intended to kill him. He answered me they would not. He being a little cheered with that, I asked him about the welfare of my husband. He told me he saw him such a time in the Bay and he was well but very melancholy. By which I certainly understood (though I suspected it before) that whatsoever the Indians told me respecting him was vanity and lies. Some of them told me he was dead and they had killed him; some said he was married again, and that the governor wished him to marry and told him he should have his choice and that all [were] persuaded I was dead. So like were these barbarous creatures to him [i.e., the devil] who was a liar from the beginning.

As I was sitting once in a wigwam here, Philip's maid came in with the child in her arms and asked me to give her a piece of my apron to make a flap; I told her I would not. Then my mistress had me give it, but still I said no. The maid told me if I would not give her a piece she would tear a piece off it. I told her I would tear her coat; then with that my mistress

[33] This was the return of a scouting party which killed three careless citizens at Hockanum, and captured Read, who escaped May 15.

rises up and takes up a stick big enough to have killed me, and struck at me with it, but I stepped out and she struck the stick into the mat of the wigwam. But while she was pulling of it out, I ran to the maid and gave her all my apron, and so that storm went over.

Hearing that my son was come to this place I went to see him and told him his father was well but very melancholy. He told me he was as much grieved for his father as for himself. I wondered at his speech for I thought I had enough upon my spirit in reference to myself to make me mindless of my husband and everyone else, they being fast among their friends. He told me also, that a while before, his master (together with other Indians) were going to the French for powder, but by the way the Mohawks met with them and killed four of their company which made the rest turn back again, for which I desire that myself and he may bless the Lord; for it might have been worse with him, had he been sold to the French, than it proved to be in his remaining with the Indians.

I went to see an English youth in this place, one John Gilbert of Springfield.[34] I found him lying without doors, upon the ground. I asked him how he did. He told me he was very sick of a flux with eating so much blood. They had turned him out of the wigwam and with him an Indian papoose, almost dead, (whose parents had been killed,) in a bitter cold day without fire or clothes. The young man himself had nothing on but his shirt and waistcoat. This sight was enough

[34] A youth of seventeen years captured about March 1.

to melt a heart of flint. There they lay quivering in the cold, the youth round like a dog, and yet alive and groaning. I advised John to go and get some fire: he told me that he could not stand, but I persuaded him still, lest he should lie there and die; and with much ado I got him to a fire and went myself home. As soon as I was got home his master's daughter came after me to know what I had done with the Englishman. I told her I had got him to a fire in such a place. Now I need to pray Paul's prayer, II Thess. iii. 2, *That we may be delivered from unreasonable and wicked men*. For her satisfaction I went along with her and brought her to him, but before I got home again it was noised about that I was running away and getting the English youth along with me; [so] that as soon as I came in they began to rant and domineer asking me where I had been and what I had been doing, and saying they would knock him on the head. I told them I had been seeing the English youth, and that I would not run away. They told me I lied, and taking up a hatchet they came to me and said they would knock me down if I stirred out again, and so confined me to the wigwam. Now may I say with David, II Sam. xxiv. 14, *I am in a great strait*. If I keep in I must die with hunger and if I go out I must be knocked in the head. This distressed condition held that day and half the next; and then the Lord remembered me, whose mercies are great. Then came an Indian to me with a pair of stockings that were too big for him, and he would have me ravel them out and knit them fit for him. I showed myself willing and bid him ask my mistress if I might go along with him a little way. She said yes I might, but I was not a little refreshed with that news that I had my liberty again. Then I went along with him and he gave me some roasted ground-nuts which did again revive my feeble stomach.

Being got out of her sight I had time and liberty again to look into my Bible which was my guide by day and my pillow by night. Now that comfortable scripture presented itself to me, Isaiah, liv. 7, *For a small moment have I forsaken thee, but with great mercies will I gather thee.* Thus the Lord carried me along from one time to another and made good to me his precious promise and many others. Then my son came to see me and I asked his master to let him stay a while with me that I might comb his head and look over him for he was almost overcome with lice. He told me when I had done that he was very hungry, but I had nothing to relieve him; but bid him go into the wigwams as he went along and see if he could get anything among them. Which he did, and it seems tarried a little too long, for his master was angry with him and beat him and then sold him. Then he came running to tell me he had a new master, and that he had given him some ground-nuts already. Then I went along with him to his new master who told me he loved him and he should not want. So his master carried him away and I never saw him afterwards till I saw him at Piscataqua in Portsmouth.

That night they bade me go out of the wigwam again. My mistress's papoose was sick and it died that night; and there was one benefit in it, that there was more room. I went to a wigwam and they bade me come in and gave me a skin to lie upon and a mess of venison and ground-nuts, which was a choice dish among them. On the morrow they buried the papoose, and afterwards, both morning and evening, there came a company to mourn and howl with her, though I confess I could not much console with them. Many sorrowful days I had in this place, often getting alone, *Like a crane or a swallow, so did I chatter; I did mourn as a dove, mine eyes fail with looking upward. O Lord, I am oppressed, undertake for me.* Isaiah xxxviii. 14. I could tell the Lord as Hezekiah [did], verse 3. *Remember now O Lord, I beseech thee, how I have walked before thee in truth.* — Now had I time to examine all my ways: my conscience did not accuse me of unrighteousness towards one or another; yet I saw how in my walk with God I had been a careless creature. As David said, *Against thee, thee only have I sinned.* And I might say with the poor publican, *God be merciful unto me a sinner.* On the Sabbath-days I could look upon the sun, and think how people were going to the house of God to have their souls refreshed and then home, and their bodies also; but I was destitute of both, and might say as the poor prodigal, *He would fain have filled his belly with the husks that the swine did eat, and no man gave unto him,* Luke xv. 16. For I must say with him *Father I have sinned against heaven and in thy sight*, verse 21. I remember how on the night before and after the Sabbath, when my family was about me, and relations and neighbors with us, we could pray and sing, and then refresh our bodies with the good creatures of God, and then have a comfortable bed to lie down on; but instead of all this, I had only a little swill for the body, and then, like a swine, must lie down on the ground. I cannot express to man the sorrow that lay upon my spirit, the Lord knows it. Yet that comfortable scripture would often come to my mind, *For a small moment have I forsaken thee, but with great mercies will I gather thee.*

THE FOURTEENTH REMOVE [35]

Now must we pack up and be gone from this thicket, bending our course toward the Bay-towns, I having nothing to eat by the way this day but a few crumbs of cake that an Indian gave my girl the same day we were taken. She gave it me and I put it in my pocket; there it lay till it was so mouldy (for want of good baking) that one could not tell what it was made of. It fell all to crumbs and grew so dry and hard that it

[35] This was probably about April 20. When the news of Canonchet's death reached the Indians, they became thoroughly disheartened. They were without ammunition, decimated by disease, and threatened with starvation. The western Indians put no trust in Philip's capacity or courage, revolted from his command, and even threatened to send his head to Boston. The Nashaways and Quabaugs left for Wachusett about April 10, and Philip and Quanopin went with them. Their squaws and children remained awhile in the neighborhood of the Connecticut, living precariously upon wild roots and game.

was like little flints, and this refreshed me many times when I was ready to faint. It was in my thoughts when I put it into my mouth, that if ever I returned, I would tell the world what a blessing the Lord gave to such mean food. As we went along they killed a deer with a young one in her. They gave me a piece of the fawn and it was so young and tender that one might eat the bones as well as the flesh, and yet I thought it very good. When night came on we sat down. It rained but they quickly got up a bark wigwam where I lay dry that night. I looked out in the morning and many of them had lain in the rain all night, I saw by their reeking. Thus the Lord dealt mercifully with me many times and I fared better than many of them. In the morning they took the blood of the deer and put it into the paunch and so boiled it. I could eat nothing of that, though they ate it sweetly. And yet they were so nice in other things that when I had fetched water and had put the dish I dipped the water with into the kettle of water which I brought they would say they would knock me down; for they said it was a sluttish trick.

The Fifteenth Remove [36]

We went on our travel. I having got one handful of ground-nuts for my support that day, they gave me my load and I went on cheerfully (with the thoughts of going homeward) having my burden more on my

[36] Camp on Miller's River at the crossing in Orange, near the Athol line.

back than my spirit. We came to the Baquag river again that day, near which we abode a few days. Sometimes one of them would give me a pipe, another a little tobacco, another a little salt, which I would change for a little victuals. I cannot but think what a wolfish appetite persons have in a starving condition, for many times when they gave me that which was hot I was so greedy that I should burn my mouth [so] that it would trouble me hours after and yet I should quickly do the same again. And after I was thoroughly hungry I was never again satisfied. For though sometimes it fell out that I got enough and did eat until I could no more, yet I was as unsatisfied as I was when I began. And now could I see that scripture verified, (there being many scriptures which we do not take notice of, or understand, till we are afflicted) Micah vi. 14, *Thou shalt eat and not be satisfied.* Now might I see more than ever before the mercies that sin hath brought upon us. Many times I should be ready to run out against the heathen, but the scripture would quiet me again, Amos iii. 6, *Shall there be evil in the city, and the Lord hath not done it?* The Lord help me to make a right improvement of his word and that I might learn that great lesson, Micah, vi. 8, 9, *He hath showed thee, O man, what is good, and what doth the Lord require of thee but to do justly, and love mercy, and walk humbly with thy God? Hear ye the rod, and who hath appointed it?*

The Sixteenth Remove [37]

We began this remove with wading over Baquag river. The water was up to the knees and the stream very swift and so cold that I thought it would have cut me in sunder. I was so weak and feeble that I reeled as I went along and thought that I must end my days at last after my bearing and getting through so many difficulties. The Indians stood laughing to see me staggering, but in my distress the Lord gave me experience of the truth and goodness of that promise, Isaiah xliii. 2, *When thou passest through the waters I will be with thee, and through the rivers, they shall not overflow thee.* Then I sat down to put on my stockings and shoes, with the tears running down mine eyes and many sorrowful thoughts in my heart, but I gat up to go along with them. Quickly there came up to us an Indian who informed them that I must go to Wachusett to my master, for there was a letter come from the Council to the Sagamores about redeeming the captives, and that there would be another in fourteen days, and that I must be ready. My heart was so heavy before that I could scarce speak or go in the path, and yet now so light that I could run. My strength seemed to come again and recruit my feeble knees and aching heart, yet it pleased them to go but one mile that night, and there we stayed two days. In that time came a company of Indians to us, nearly thirty, all on horse-back. My heart skipped within

[37] Camp about one mile south of Miller's River, near the Orange and Athol line.

me thinking they had been Englishmen, at the first sight of them, for they were dressed in English apparel, with hats, white neck-cloths, and sashes about their waists, and ribbons upon their shoulders; but when they came near, there was a vast difference between the lovely faces of Christians, and the foul looks of those heathens, which much dampened my spirit again.

The Seventeenth Remove [38]

A comfortable remove it was to me because of my hopes. They gave me a pack and along we went cheerfully. But quickly my will proved more than my strength. Having little or no refreshing, my strength failed me and my spirit was almost gone. Now may I say with David, Psalm cix. 22, 23, 24, *I am poor and needy, and my heart is wounded within me. I am gone like the shadow when it declineth; I am tossed up and down like the locust: my knees are weak through fasting, and my flesh faileth of fatness.* At night we came to an Indian town, and the Indians sat down by a wigwam, discoursing, but I was almost spent and could scarce speak. I laid down my load and went into a wigwam and there sat an Indian boiling of horses' feet (they being wont to eat the flesh first, and when the feet were old and dried and they had nothing else, they would cut off the feet and use them.) I asked him to give me a little of his broth or water they

[38] Camp probably at the Indian village of Nichewaug in Petersham.

were boiling in. He took a dish and gave me one spoonful of samp and bid me take as much broth as I would. Then I put some of the hot water to the samp and drank it up and my spirit came again. He gave me also a piece of the ruff or ridding of the small guts and I broiled it on the coals. And now may I say with Jonathan, *See, I pray you, how mine eyes have been enlightened, because I tasted a little of this honey.* I Sam. xiv. 29. Now is my spirit revived again; though means be never so inconsiderable, yet if the Lord bestow his blessing upon them, they shall refresh both soul and body.

THE EIGHTEENTH REMOVE [39]

We took up our packs and along we went but a wearisome day I had of it. As we went along I saw an Englishman stripped naked and lying dead upon the ground, but knew not who it was. Then we came to another Indian town where we stayed all night. In this town there were four English children, captives, and one of them my own sister's. I went to see how she did and she was well considering her captive condition. I would have tarried that night with her, but they that owned her would not suffer it. Then I went into another wigwam where they were boiling corn and beans, which was a lovely sight to see, but I could not get a taste thereof. Then I went to another wigwam where there were two of the English children;

[39] Camp at an Indian village near Menameset, probably on Barre Plains.

the squaw was boiling horse's feet; then she cut me
off a little piece and gave one of the English children
a piece also. Being very hungry I had quickly eaten
up mine but the child could not bite it, it was so
tough and sinewy, but lay sucking, gnawing, chewing
and slabbering of it in the mouth and hand: then I
took it of the child and ate it myself, and savory it
was to my taste. Then I may say as Job, chapter vi.
7. *The things that my soul refused to touch, are as my
sorrowful meat.* Thus the Lord made that pleasant
and refreshing which at another time would have
been an abomination. Then I went home to my mistress's wigwam and they told me I had disgraced my
master with begging and if I did so any more they
would knock me in the head. I told them they had as
good knock me in head as starve me to death.

THE NINETEENTH REMOVE [40]

They said, when we went out, that we must travel
to Wachusett this day. But a bitter weary day I had
of it, travelling now three days together, without rest-
ing any day between. At last, after many weary
steps, I saw Wachusett hills, but many miles off.
Then we came to a great swamp through which we
travelled up to the knees in mud and water, which
was heavy going to one tired before. Being almost
spent I thought I should have sunk down at last and
never get out; but I may say, as in Psalm xciv. 18,
When my foot slipped, thy mercy, O Lord, held me up.

[40] Camp on the western side of Wachusett, probably in Princeton.

Going along, having indeed my life but little spirit, Philip who was in the company came up and took me by the hand and said: "Two weeks more and you shall be Mistress again." I asked him if he spake true. He answered, "Yes, and quickly you shall come to your master again," who had been gone from us three weeks. After many weary steps we came to Wachusett where he was, and glad I was to see him. He asked me when I washed me [last.] I told him not this month. Then he fetched me some water himself and bid me wash and gave me a glass to see how I looked and bid his squaw give me something to eat. So she gave me a mess of beans and meat and a little ground-nut cake. I was wonderfully revived with this favor showed me. Psalm cvi. 46, *He made them also to be pitied of all those that carried them captives.*

My master had three squaws,[41] living sometimes with one, and sometimes with another. One [was] this old squaw, at whose wigwam I was, and with whom my master had been those three weeks. Another was Weetamoo, with whom I had lived and served all this while. A severe and proud dame she was; bestowing every day, in dressing herself neat, as

[41] Quanopin, Mrs. Rowlandson's purchaser, was a Narraganset and the grandnephew of Canonicus. His oldest squaw was Onux; his second, whom Mrs. Rowlandson served as maid, was Weetamoo, Queen of Pocasset and sister-in-law of Philip; being the sister of his wife and also the widow of his brother Alexander, *alias* Wamsutta. Quanopin was her third husband. She was drowned in attempting to swim across the river or arm of the sea at Mattapoisett to escape capture. Quanopin was captured, tried at Newport, and shot August 25, 1676.

much time as any of the gentry of the land, powdering her hair and painting her face, going with necklaces, with jewels in her ears, and bracelets upon her hands. When she had dressed herself, her work was to make girdles of wampum and beads. The third squaw was a younger one by whom he had two papooses. By that time I was refreshed by the old squaw, with whom my master was. Weetamoo's maid came to call me home, at which I fell a weeping. Then the old squaw told me, to encourage me, that if I wanted victuals, I should come to her and that I should lie there in her wigwam. Then I went with the maid and quickly came again and lodged there. The squaw laid a mat under me and a good rug over me: the first time I had any such kindness showed me. I understood that Weetamoo thought that if she let me go and serve with the old squaw, she would be in danger to lose, not only my service, but the redemption-pay also. And I was not a little glad to hear this; being by it raised in my hopes that in God's due time there would be an end of this sorrowful hour. Then came an Indian and asked me to knit him three pairs of stockings for which I had a hat and a silk handkerchief. Then another asked me to make her a shirt for which she gave me an apron.

Then came Tom and Peter [42] with the second letter

[42] Tom Dublet and Peter Conway were Christian Indians of Nashobah, who, upon repeated petitions from Mr. Rowlandson and other clergymen to the Council, were persuaded to serve as messengers to the hostile sachems, seeking the terms upon which they would release the captives. Dublet's first visit to them, which he

from the Council about the captives. Though they
were Indians I took them by the hand and burst out
into tears. My heart was so full that I could not
speak to them; but recovering myself, I asked them
how my husband did, and all my friends and ac-
quaintances. They said, "They are all very well, but
melancholy." They brought me two bisquits and a
pound of tobacco. The tobacco I quickly gave away.
When it was all gone, one asked me to give him a pipe
of tobacco. I told him it was all gone. Then he began

made alone, was on April 3. On his second visit Dublet was accompanied by Peter, bearing a letter from the Council. They
brought back, on April 27, a reply from the chiefs, written by James
Printer, an Indian who had served sixteen years' apprenticeship in
Samuel Green's printing office at Cambridge. Mr. John Hoar, of
Concord, accompanied Dublet upon his third journey to Wachusett, carrying the ransom for Mrs. Rowlandson in money and goods
raised by several Boston gentlemen, and happily effected her release. On Monday, May 7, Dublet with Seth Perry was again
sent to the sachems by the Council. A verbal message seems to
have been returned appointing a meeting, and Jonathan Prescott
was sent the following Thursday to make arrangements. The pro-
posed meeting was held between Groton and Concord, and then or
soon after several captives were ransomed, or released uncondition-
ally. June 7, under guidance of Tom Dublet, Captain Daniel
Henchman surprised a party of Indians fishing in the Washacum
ponds. They were chiefly women and children. Seven were killed
and twenty-nine were captured. These prisoners with others were
ultimately sent to the West Indies and sold as slaves. This hum-
bling blow and the increasing difficulty of obtaining subsistence
turned the boasting of the proud sachems to a despairing desire for
peace. The sole reward by which the Massachusetts Colony recog-
nized the services rendered by the brave copper-colored Christian,
Thomas Dublet, was "two coats," voted him, upon petition, by the
Council eight years later. The text of these letters is to be found in
full in the edition of Messrs. Nourse and Thayer, 1903.

to rant and threaten. I told him when my husband came I would give him some. "Hang him, rogue," says he, "I will knock out his brains if he comes here." And then again, in the same breath, they would say that if there should come an hundred without guns, they would do them no hurt. So unstable and like mad-men they were. So that, fearing the worst, I durst not send to my husband, though there were some thoughts of his coming to redeem and fetch me, not knowing what might follow, for there was little more trust to them than to the master they served. When the letter was come, the sagamores met to consult about the captives and called me to them to inquire how much my husband would give to redeem me. When I came I sat down among them as I was wont to do, as their manner is. Then they bade me stand up and said they were the General Court. They bid me speak what I thought he would give. Now knowing that all we had was destroyed by the Indians, I was in a great strait. I thought if I should speak but a little it would be slighted and hinder the matter; if of a great sum, I knew not where it would be procured. Yet at a venture I said twenty pounds, yet desired them to take less. But they would not hear of that, but sent that message to Boston, that for twenty pounds I should be redeemed. It was a praying-Indian that wrote their letter for them.

There was another praying Indian who told me that he had a brother that would not eat horse, his conscience was so tender and scrupulous (though

large as hell for the destruction of poor Christians.)
Then he said he read that scripture to him, II Kings,
vi. 25. *There was a famine in Samaria, and behold they
besieged it, until an ass's head was sold for four-score
pieces of silver, and the fourth part of a kab of dove's dung
for five pieces of silver.* He expounded this place to his
brother and showed him that it was lawful to eat that
in a famine which is not at another time, and now,
says he, he will eat horse with any Indian of them all.
There was another praying Indian, who when he had
done all the mischief that he could, betrayed his own
father into the English hands, thereby to purchase
his own life. Another praying Indian was at Sudbury
fight,[43] though, as he deserved, he was afterwards
hanged for it. There was another praying Indian, so
wicked and cruel as to wear a string about his neck,
strung with Christian's fingers. Another praying
Indian, when they went to Sudbury fight, went with
them, and his squaw also with him with her papoose
at her back. Before they went to that fight they got a
company together to powwow. The manner was as
followeth:

There was one that kneeled upon a deer-skin, with
the company round him in a ring, who kneeled, and
striking upon the ground with their hands and with
sticks and muttering or humming with their mouths.

[43] This was on April 18, when the brave Captains Samuel Wadsworth, of Milton, and Samuel Brocklebank, of Rowley, with thirty
or more of their men, were slain, having been drawn into an am-
bush.

Besides him who kneeled in the ring, there also stood
one with a gun in his hand. Then he on the deer-skin
made a speech and all manifested assent to it, and so
they did many times together. Then they bid him
with a gun go out of the ring, which he did; but when
he was out they called him in again, but he seemed to
make a stand; then they called the more earnestly until he returned again. Then they all sang. Then they
gave him two guns; in either hand, one. And so he on
the deer-skin began again. And at the end of every
sentence in his speaking they all assented, humming
or muttering with their mouths and striking upon the
ground with their hands. Then they bade him with
the two guns go out of the ring again, which he did,
a little way. Then they called him in again, but he
made a stand; so they called him with greater earnest-
ness. But he stood reeling and wavering as if he knew
not whether he should stand or fall or which way to
go. Then they called him with exceeding great ve-
hemency, all of them, one and another. After a little
while he turned in, staggering as he went, with his
arms stretched out, in either hand a gun. As soon as
he came in they all rejoiced exceedingly a while, and
then he upon the deer-skin made another speech, unto
which they all assented in a rejoicing manner. And so
they ended their business and forthwith went to Sudbury fight.

To my thinking they went without any scruple but
that they should prosper and gain the victory. And
they went out not so rejoicing, but they came home

with as great a victory. For they said they had killed
two captains and almost an hundred men. One Englishman they brought along with them. And he said
it was too true, for they had made sad work at Sudbury, as indeed it proved. Yet they came home without that rejoicing and triumphing over their victory,
which they were wont to show at other times, but
rather like dogs, as they say, which have lost their
ears. Yet I could not perceive it was for their own loss
of men. They said they had not lost above five or six,
and I missed none except in one wigwam. When they
went they acted as if the devil had told them that
they should gain the victory; and now they acted as if
the devil had told them they should have a fall.
Whether it were so or no, I cannot tell, but so it proved
for quickly they began to fall and so held on that
summer till they came to utter ruin. They came home
on a Sabbath day, and the powwow that kneeled
upon the deer-skin home (I may say without abuse)
as black as the devil. When my master came home he
came to me and bid me make a shirt for his papoose, of
a holland laced pillow-beer. About that time there
came an Indian and bid me come to his wigwam at
night and he would give me some pork and ground-
nuts. Which I did and as I was eating another Indian
said to me: He seems to be your good friend, but he
killed two Englishmen at Sudbury and there lie their
clothes behind you. I looked behind me and there I
saw bloody clothes with bullet holes in them. Yet the
Lord suffered not this wretch to do me any hurt. Yea,

instead of that, he many times refreshed me: five or six times did he and his squaw refresh my feeble carcass. If I went to their wigwam at any time they would always give me something and yet they were strangers that I never saw before. Another squaw gave me a piece of fresh pork and a little salt with it and lent me her pan to fry it in; and I cannot but remember what a sweet, pleasant and delightful relish that bit had to me, to this day. So little do we prize common mercies when we have them to the full!

THE TWENTIETH REMOVE [44]

It was their usual manner to remove when they had done any mischief, lest they should be found out; and so they did at this time. We went about three or four miles and there built a great wigwam, big enough

[44] Friday, April 28, to May 2. This encampment was upon the western base of the mountain very near the southern end of Wachusett Lake. Tradition has located the final conference of John Hoar and the sachems at an isolated granite ledge near the Westminster line in Princeton, which is now known as Redemption Rock. This was bought in 1879 by the Honorable George Frisbie Hoar, and on its perpendicular face he has had the following legend inscribed:

UPON THIS ROCK MAY 2ND 1676

WAS MADE THE AGREEMENT FOR THE RANSOM

OF MRS. MARY ROWLANDSON OF LANCASTER

BETWEEN THE INDIANS AND JOHN HOAR OF CONCORD

KING PHILIP WAS WITH THE INDIANS BUT

REFUSED HIS CONSENT

REDEMPTION ROCK, PRINCETON

to hold an hundred Indians, which they did in prepa-
ration to a great day of dancing. They would say now
amongst themselves that the Governor would be so
angry for his loss at Sudbury that they would send no
more about the captives, which made me grieve and
tremble. My sister being not far from the place
where we now were, and hearing that I was here, desired her master to let her come and see me, and he
was willing to it and would go with her. But she being
ready before him, told him she would go before and
was come within a mile or two of the place. Then he
overtook her and began to rant as if he had been mad;
and made her go back again in the rain, so that I never
saw her till I saw her in Charlestown. But the Lord
requited many of their ill doings, for this Indian, her
master, was hanged afterwards in Boston.[45] The
Indians now began to come from all quarters against
their merry dancing day. Among some of them came
one Goodwife Kettle. I told her my heart was so
heavy that it was ready to break. "So is mine too,"
said she, but yet said, "I hope we shall hear some good
news shortly." I could hear how earnestly my sister
desired to see me and I as earnestly desired to see
her; and yet neither of us could get an opportunity.
My daughter was also now about a mile off and I had
not seen her in nine or ten weeks as I had not seen my
sister since our first taking. I earnestly desired them
to let me go and see them; yea, I entreated, begged,

[45] Mrs. Divoll's captor was Sagamore Sam, chief of the Nashaways, hanged at town's end, Boston, Tuesday, September 26, 1676.

and persuaded them but to let me see my daughter; and yet so hard-hearted were they, that they would not suffer it. They made use of their tyrannical power whilst they had it, but through the Lord's wonderful mercy, their time now was short.

On a Sabbath-day, the sun being about an hour high in the afternoon, came Mr. John Hoar,[46] (the Council permitting him, and his own forward spirit inclining him,) together with the two aforementioned Indians, Tom and Peter, with their third letter from the Council. When they came, I was abroad; they presently called me in and bade me sit down and not stir. Then they catched up their guns and away they ran, as if an enemy had been at hand, and the guns went off apace. I manifested some great trouble and they asked me what was the matter. I told them I thought they had killed the Englishman, (for they had in the meantime informed me that an Englishman was come.) They said no; they shot over his horse, and under and before his horse; and they pushed him this way and that way, at their pleasure, showing what they could do. Then they let them come to their wigwams. I begged them to let me see the Englishman, but they would not; but there was I, fain to sit their pleasure. When they had talked their fill to him, they suffered me to go to him. We asked each other of our welfare, and how my husband did,

---

[46] Mr. Rowlandson besought John Hoar, of Concord, to aid him in ransoming his wife, knowing him to be held in great respect by the Indians because of his many friendly services to them.

and all my friends. He told me they were all well and would be glad to see me. Amongst other things which my husband sent me, there came a pound of tobacco, which I sold for nine shillings in money; for, many of the Indians for want of tobacco smoked hemlock and ground-ivy. It was a great mistake in any who thought I sent for tobacco, for through the favor of God that desire was overcome. I now asked them whether I should go home with Mr. Hoar. They answered no, one and another of them, and it being night we laid down with that answer. In the morning Mr. Hoar invited the sagamores to dinner, but when we went to get it ready, we found that they had stolen the greatest part of the provisions Mr. Hoar had brought, out of his bags, in the night. And we may see the wonderful power of God in that one passage, in that when there was such a great number of Indians together and so greedy of a little food, and no English there but Mr. Hoar and myself, that there they did not knock us in the head and take what we had, there being not only some provisions but trading-cloth, a part of the twenty pounds agreed upon. But instead of doing us any mischief they seemed to be ashamed of the fact and said it were some Machit Indians [47] that did it. Oh, that we could believe that there is nothing too hard for God! God showed his power over the heathen in this, as he did over the hungry lions when Daniel was cast into the den. Mr. Hoar called them betimes to dinner, but they ate

[47] That is, bad Indians.

very little, they being so busy in dressing themselves, and getting ready for their dance, which was carried on by eight of them, four men and four squaws, my master and his mistress being two. He was dressed in his Holland shirt with great laces sewed at the tail of it. He had his silver buttons, his white stockings, his garters were hung round with shillings and he had girdles of wampum upon his head and shoulders. She had a jersey coat, and covered with girdles of wampum from the loins upward; her arms from her elbows to her hands were covered with bracelets; there were handfuls of necklaces about her neck and several sorts of jewels in her ears. She had fine red stockings and white shoes, her hair powdered and her face painted red, that was always before, black. And all the dancers were after the same manner. There were two others singing and knocking on a kettle for their music. They kept hopping up and down, one after another, with a kettle of water in the midst, standing warm upon some embers, to drink of when they were dry. They held on till it was almost night throwing out wampum to the standers-by. At night I asked them again if I should go home. They all as one said no, except my husband come for me. When we were lain down my master went out of the wigwam, and by and by sent in an Indian called James the Printer, who told Mr. Hoar, that my master would let me go tomorrow if he would let him have one pint of liquors. Then Mr. Hoar called his own Indians, Tom and Peter, and bid them go and see whether he would promise it before them three, and if he would he should have it; which he did, and he had it. Then Philip smelling the business called me to him and asked me what I would give him to tell me some good news and speak a good word for me. I told him I could not tell what to give him; I would [give him] anything I had, and asked him what he would have. He said two coats and twenty shillings in money and half a bushel of feed corn and some tobacco. I thanked him for his love, but I knew the good news as well as the crafty fox. My master, after he had had his drink, quickly came ranting into the wigwam again, and called for Mr. Hoar, drinking to him and saying he was a good man, and then again he would say, hang him, rogue. Being almost drunk he would drink to him and yet presently say he should be hanged. Then he called for me. I trembled to hear him, yet I was fain to go to him, and he drank to me showing no incivility. He was the first Indian I saw drunk all the while that I was amongst them. At last his squaw ran out and he after her round the wigwam with his money jingling at his knees. But she escaped him, but having an old squaw he ran to her, and lo, through the Lord's mercy, we were no more troubled that night. Yet I had not a comfortable night's rest, for I think I can say, I did not sleep for three nights together. The night before the letter came from the Council I could not rest I was so full of fears and troubles, God many times leaving us most in the dark when deliverance is nearest; yea, at this time I could not rest night nor day. The next night I was overjoyed, Mr. Hoar being come, and that with such good tidings. The third night I was even swallowed up with the thoughts of things, viz., that ever I should go home again; and that I must go leaving my children behind me in the wilderness; so that sleep was now almost departed from mine eyes.

On Tuesday morning they called their General Court (as they call it) to consult and determine whether I should go home or no. And they all as one man did seemingly consent to it, that I should go home, except Philip, who would not come among them.

But before I go any further, I would take leave to mention a few remarkable passages of providence, which I took special notice of in my affliction.

1. Of the fair opportunity lost in the long march a little after the Fort Fight when our English army was so numerous, and in pursuit of the enemy, and so near as to take several and destroy them; and the enemy in such distress for food that our men might track them by their rooting in the earth for ground-nuts whilst they were flying for their lives. I say that then our Army should want provision, and be forced to leave their pursuit and return homeward; and the very next week the enemy came upon our town like bears bereft of their whelps or so many ravenous wolves, rending us and our lambs to death. But what shall I say? God seemed to leave his people to themselves and order all things for his own holy ends. *Shall there*

*be evil in the city and the Lord hath not done it? They
are not grieved for the affliction of Joseph, therefore shall
they go captive, with the first that go captive.* It is the
Lord's doing and it should be marvelous in our eyes.

2. I cannot but remember how the Indians derided
the slowness and dullness of the English army in its
setting out. For after the desolations of Lancaster
and Medfield as I went along with them they asked
me when I thought the English army would come after
them. I told them I could not tell. "It may be they
will come in May," said they. Thus did they scoff at
us, as if the English would be a quarter of a year
getting ready.

3. Which also I have hinted before, when the English army with new supplies were sent forth to pursue
after the enemy, and they understanding it, fled before them till they came to Baquag River, where they
forthwith went over safely: that that river should be
impassable to the English. I can but admire to see
the wonderful providence of God in preserving the
heathen for farther affliction to our poor country.
They could go in great numbers over, but the English
must stop! God had an overruling hand in all those
things.

4. It was thought, if the corn were cut down, they
would starve and die with hunger; and all their corn
that could be found was destroyed and they driven
from the little they had in store into the woods in the
midst of winter; and yet how to admiration did the
Lord preserve them for his holy ends, and the destruc-

tion of many still amongst the English! Strangely did
the Lord provide for them, that I did not see (all the
time I was among them) one man, woman or child, die
with hunger.

Though many times they would eat that, that a hog
or dog would hardly touch, yet by that, God strength-
ened them to be a scourge to his people.

The chief and commonest food was ground-nuts.
They eat also nuts and acorns, artichokes, lily-roots,
ground-beans, and several other weeds and roots that
I know not.

They would pick up old bones and cut them to
pieces at the joints, and if they were full of worms and
magots they would scald them over the fire to make
the vermine come out, and then boil them and drink
up the liquor, and then beat the great ends of them in
a morter, and so eat them. They would eat horses'
guts and ears and all sorts of wild birds which they
would catch: also bear, venison, beaver, tortoise, frogs,
squirrels, dogs, skunks, rattle-snakes, yea, the very
bark of trees, besides all sorts of creatures and provisions which they plundered from the English. I can
but stand in admiration to see the wonderful power
of God in providing for such a vast number of enemies
in the wilderness where there was nothing to be seen,
but from hand to mouth. Many times in a morning
the generality of them would eat up all they had and
yet have some farther supply against they wanted.
It is said, Psalm lxxxi. 13, 14, *Oh that my people had
hearkened to me and Israel had walked in my ways, I*

should soon have subdued their enemies, and turned my hand against their adversaries. But now our perverse and evil carriages in the sight of the Lord have so offended him that instead of turning his hand against them, the Lord feeds and nourishes them up to be a scourge to the whole land.

5. Another thing that I would observe is, the strange providence of God in turning things about when the Indians were at the highest, and the English at the lowest. I was with the enemy eleven weeks and five days, and not one week passed without the fury of the enemy, and some desolation by fire and sword upon some place or other. They mourned (with their blackened faces) for their own losses yet triumphed and rejoiced in their inhumane and many times devilish cruelty to the English. They would boast much of their victories, saying that in two hours time they had destroyed such a captain and his company at such a place, and such a captain and his company in such a place, and such a captain in such a place; and boast how many towns they had destroyed, and then scoff and say they had done them a good turn to send them to Heaven so soon. Again they would say this summer that they would knock all the rogues in the head or drive them into the sea or make them flee the country, thinking surely, Agag-like, *the bitterness of death is past.* Now the heathen begin to think all is their own; and the poor Christian hopes to fail (as to man) and now their eyes are more on God and their hearts sigh heavenward, and so say in good earnest, *Help,*

Lord or we perish. When the Lord had brought his
people to this, that they saw no help in anything but
himself, then he takes the quarrel into his own hand,
and though they [i.e., the Indians] had made a pit (in
their own imaginations) as deep as hell for the Christians that summer, yet the Lord hurled themselves
into it. And the Lord had not so many ways before to
preserve them but now he hath as many to destroy
them.

But to return again to my going home, where we
may see a remarkable change of providence. At first
they were all against it except my husband would
come for me, but afterwards they assented to it and
seemed much to rejoice in it. Some asked me to send
them some bread, others some tobacco, others shak-
ing me by the hand offering me a hood and scarfe to
ride in; not one moving hand or tongue against it.
Thus hath the Lord answered my poor desire and the
many earnest requests of others put up unto God for
me. In my travels an Indian came to me and told me
if I were willing he and his squaw would run away and
go home along with me. I told him no; I was not willing to run away but desired to wait God's time that I
might go home quietly and without fear. And now
God hath granted me my desire. O the wonderful
power of God that I have seen and the experience that
I have had. I have been in the midst of those roaring
lions and savage bears that feared neither God nor
man nor the devil, by night and day, alone and in
company, sleeping all sorts together, and yet not one

of them ever offered me the least abuse of unchastity to me in word or action. Though some are ready to say, I speak it for my own credit; but I speak it in the presence of God, and to his glory. God's power is as great now, and as sufficient to save, as when he preserved Daniel in the lion's den, or the three children in the fiery furnace. I may well say as his Psalm cvii. 12, *Oh give thanks unto the Lord for he is good for his mercy endureth for ever.* Let the redeemed of the Lord say so, whom he hath redeemed from the hand of the enemy, especially that I should have come away in the midst of so many hundreds of enemies, quietly and peacefully, and not a dog moving his tongue. So I took my leave of them and in coming along my heart melted into tears more than all the while I was with them and I was almost swallowed up with the thoughts that ever I should go home again. About the sun going down, Mr. Hoar and myself and the two Indians came to Lancaster and a solemn sight it was to me. There had I lived many comfortable years amongst my relations and neighbors, and now not one Christian to be seen nor one house left standing. We went on to a farm-house [48] that was yet standing, where we lay all night; and a comfortable lodging we had, though nothing but straw to lie on. The Lord preserved us in safety that night and raised us up again in the morn-

[48] This dwelling was probably on the trail to Marlborough, where Ensign John Moore and one or two others had their homes. "Not one house was left standing" in Lancaster, not even the meeting-house.

ing and carried us along; thus before noon we came to Concord. Now was I full of joy and yet not without sorrow; joy to see such a lovely sight, so many Christians together and some of my neighbors. There I met with my brother and my brother-in-law [49] who asked me if I knew where his wife was. Poor heart, he had helped to bury her and knew it not, she being shot down by the house, was partly burned, so that those who were at Boston at the desolation of the town and came back afterwards and buried the dead, did not know her. Yet I was not without sorrow to think how many were looking and longing, and my own children among the rest, to enjoy that deliverance that I had now received, and I did not know whether ever I should see them again. Being recruited with food and raiment we went to Boston that day where I met with my dear husband, but the thoughts of our dear children, one being dead, and the other we could not tell where, abated our comfort each to other. I was not before so much hemmed in with the merciless and cruel heathen, but now as much with pitiful, tender-hearted and compassionate Christians. In that poor and distressed and beggerly condition I was received in, I was kindly entertained in several houses: so much love I received from several (some of whom I knew, and others I knew not) that I am not capable to declare it. But the Lord knows them all by name; the Lord reward them seven-fold into their bosoms of his spirituals for their temporals.

[49] Josiah White and Lieutenant Henry Kerley.

The twenty pounds, the price of my redemption, was raised by some Boston gentlemen, and Mr. Usher,[50] whose bounty and religious charity, I would not forget to make mention of. Then Mr. Thomas Shepard of Charlestown received us into his house where we continued eleven weeks; and a father and mother they were to us. And many more tender-hearted friends we met with in that place. We were now in the midst of love, yet not without much and frequent heaviness of heart for our poor children and other relations who were still in affliction. The week following, after my coming in, the Governor and the Council sent forth to the Indians again, and that not without success, for they brought in my sister and good-wife Kettle. Their not knowing where our children were, was a sore trial to us still, and yet we were not without secret hopes that we should see them again. That which was dead lay heavier upon my spirit than those which were living and amongst the heathen, thinking how it suffered with its wounds and I was no way able to relieve it, and how it was buried by the heathens in the wilderness from among all Christians. We were hurried up and down in our thoughts, sometimes we should hear a report that they had gone this way, and sometimes that. We kept inquiring and listening to hear concerning them, but no certain news as yet. About this time the Council had ordered a day of public thanksgiving, though I thought I still had cause for mourn-

---

[50] Hezekiah Usher was a prominent and wealthy merchant and one of the selectmen, living on what is now State Street, Boston.

ing, and being unsettled in our minds, we thought we would ride toward the eastward to see if we could hear anything concerning our children. And as we were riding along (God is the wise disposer of all things) between Ipswich and Rowley we met with Mr. William Hubbard who told us that our son Joseph was come in to Major Waldron's [51] and another with him, which was my sister's son. I asked him how he knew it. He said the Major himself told him so. So along we went till we came to Newbury, and the minister there being absent, they desired my husband to preach the Thanksgiving for them. But he was not willing to stay there that night, but would go over to Salisbury, to hear further, and come again in the morning; which he did, and preached there that day. At night, when he had done, one came and told him that his daughter was come in at Providence. Here was mercy on both hands. Now hath God fulfilled that precious scripture which was such a comfort to me in my distressed condition. When my heart was ready to sink into the earth (my children being gone I could not tell whither) and my knees trembled under me, and I was walking *through the valley of the shadow of death*, then the Lord brought, and now has fulfilled, that reviving word unto me: Thus saith the Lord, *Refrain thy voice from weeping and thine eyes from tears for thy work shall be rewarded, saith the Lord, and they shall come again from the land of the enemy.* Now were we between them, the

[51] Richard Waldron, of Dover, New Hampshire, its most distinguished citizen.

one on the east, and the other on the west. Our son being nearest, we went to him first, to Portsmouth, where we met with him, and with the Major also, who told us he had done what he could, but could not redeem him under seven pounds, which the good people thereabouts were pleased to pay. The Lord reward the Major and all the rest, though unknown to me, for their labor of love. My sister's son [52] was redeemed for four pounds, which the Council gave order for the payment of. Having now received one of our children, we hastened towards the other; going back through Newbury, my husband preached there on the Sabbath-day; for which they rewarded him many fold.

On Monday we came to Charlestown where we learned that the Governor of Rhode Island had sent over for our daughter, to take care of her, being now within his jurisdiction; which should not pass without our acknowledgments. But being nearer Rehoboth than Rhode Island, Mr. Newman [53] went over, and took care of her, and brought her to his own house. And the goodness of God was admirable to us in our low estate, in that he raised up passionate friends on every side to us, when we had nothing to recompence any for their love.

The Indians were now gone that way [so] that it appeared dangerous to go to her. But the carts which carried provisions to the English army, being guarded, brought her with them to Dorchester where we re-

[52] Mrs. Hannah Divoll's.
[53] The Reverend Noah Newman of Rehoboth.

ceived her safe: blessed be the Lord for it, for great is
his power and he can do whatsoever seemeth him
good. Her coming in was after this manner: she was
travelling one day with the Indians, with her basket
at her back; the company of Indians were got before
her and gone out of sight, all except one squaw. She
followed the squaw till night and then both of them
lay down, having nothing over them but the heavens
and under them but the earth. Thus she travelled
three days together, not knowing whither she was going, having nothing to eat or drink but water and
green whortleberries. At last they came into Providence where she was kindly entertained by several of
that town. The Indians often said that I should never
have her under twenty pounds, but now the Lord
hath brought her in upon free cost and given her to
me the second time. The Lord make us a blessing indeed, each to others. Now have I seen that scripture
also fulfilled, Deut. xxx. 4, 7, *If any of thine be driven
out to the outmost parts of heaven, from thence will the
Lord thy God gather thee, and from thence will he fetch
thee. And the Lord thy God will put all these curses
upon thine enemies, and on them which hate thee, which
persecuted thee.* Thus hath the Lord brought me and
mine out of that horrible pit and hath set us in the
midst of tender-hearted and compassionate Christians. It is the desire of my soul that we may walk
worthy of the mercies received, and which we are re-
ceiving.

Our family being now gathered together (those of

us that were living) the South Church in Boston hired
an house for us. Then we removed from Mr. Shepard's
(those cordial friends) and went to Boston where we
continued about three quarters of a year. Still the
Lord went along with **us** and provided graciously for
us. I thought it somewhat strange to set up house-
keeping with bare walls, but, as Solomon says, *Money
answers all things*. And that we had through the
benevolence of Christian friends, some in this town,
and some in that, and others, and some from England,
that in a little time we might look and see the house
furnished with love. The Lord hath been exceeding
good to us in our low estate, in that when we had
neither house nor home nor other necessaries, the Lord
so moved the hearts of these and those towards us
that we wanted neither food nor raiment for our-
selves and ours, Proverbs, xviii. 24, *There is a friend
that sticketh closer than a brother*. And how many such
friends have we found, and now living amongst! And
truly such a friend have we found him to be unto us,
in whose house we lived, viz., Mr. James Whitcomb,[54]
a friend unto us near hand, and afar off.

I can remember the time when I used to sleep
quietly without working in my thoughts, whole nights
together, but now it is otherwise with me. When all
are fast about me and no eye open but his who ever
waketh, my thoughts are upon things past, upon the
awful dispensation of the Lord towards us, upon his

[54] A wealthy citizen of Boston, whose mansion and garden were
at the corner of Beacon and Tremont Streets.

wonderful power and might in carrying us through so many difficulties, in returning us to safety and suffering none to hurt us. I remember in the night season, how the other day I was in the midst of thousands of enemies and nothing but death before me. It was then hard work to persuade myself that ever I should be satisfied with bread again. But now we are fed with the finest of the wheat, and (as I may say) with *honey out of the rock*. Instead of the husk, we have the fatted calf. The thoughts of these things in the particulars of them, and of the love and goodness of God towards us, make it true of me, what David said to himself, Psalm vi. 5, *I watered my couch with my tears*. O the wonderful power of God that mine eyes have seen, affording matter enough for my thoughts to run in, that when others are sleeping mine eyes are weeping.

I have seen the extreme vanity of this world. One hour I have been in health, and wealth, wanting nothing, but the next hour in sickness, and wounds, and death, having nothing but sorrow and affliction.

Before I knew what affliction meant, I was ready sometimes to wish for it. When I lived in prosperity, having the comforts of the world about me, my relations by me, my heart cheerful, and taking little care for anything, and yet seeing many (whom I preferred before myself) under many trials and afflictions, in sickness, weakness, poverty, losses, crosses, and cares of the world, I should be sometimes jealous lest I should have my portion in this life, and that scripture would come to my mind, Hebrews xii. 6, *For whom the*

Lord loveth he chasteneth, and scourgeth every son whom he receiveth. But now I see the Lord had his time to scourge and chasten me. The portion of some is to have their affliction by drops, now one drop and then another, but the dregs of the cup, the wine of astonishment (like a sweeping rain that leaveth no food) did the Lord prepare to be my portion. Affliction I wanted, and affliction I had, full measure (I thought) pressed down and running over. Yet I see when God calls a person to anything, and through never so many difficulties, yet he is fully able to carry them through, and make them see and say they have been gainers thereby. And I hope I can say in some measure, as David did, *It is good for me that I have been afflicted.* The Lord hath showed me the vanity of these outward things; that they are the *Vanity of vanities, and vexation of spirit;* that they are but a shadow, a blast, a bubble, and things of no continuance; that we must rely on God himself, and our whole dependence must be upon him. If trouble with smaller things begin to arise in me, I have something at hand to check myself with, and say, why am I troubled? It was but the other day that if I had had the world, I would have given it for my freedom, or to have been a servant to a Christian. I have learned to look beyond present and smaller troubles, and to be quieted under them, as Moses said, Exodus xiv. 13, *Stand still and see the salvation of the Lord.*

FINIS

THE MARY ROWLANDSON LOCKER

APPENDIX

EDITIONS OF THE PRESENT WORK

1682, two at Cambridge (Massachusetts)

1682, one at London (England)

1720, Boston

1770, two at Boston

1771, Boston

1773, Boston

1773, New London (Connecticut)

1791, Boston

1792, one each at Haverhill and Amherst (New Hampshire)

1794, Boston

1795, Leominster

1800, Boston

1805, Boston

1811, Brookfield

1812, London (England)

1828, two editions at Lancaster

1831, Concord (New Hampshire)

1839–1854, several editions at Boston, Auburn, and Buffalo (New York)

1841, Concord (New Hampshire)

1842, Boston

1853, Clinton; another at Concord (New Hampshire)

1856, Boston

1857, n.p.
1859, New York
1883, New York; another at Concord (New Hampshire)
1888, New York
1900, Haverhill (Massachusetts)
1903, Lancaster (the Nourse and Thayer edition)
1930, Boston
1953, Lancaster (The Tercentenary edition)

NOTES

MARY (WHITE) ROWLANDSON was the daughter of
John and Joane (West) White, of South Petherton,
County Somerset, England, who appeared in Salem
as early as 1638, and moved from their Wenham lands
to Lancaster in 1653. John White was the wealthiest
of the original proprietors of Lancaster. He left what
would be the equivalent of about twenty thousand
dollars of our money. His wife died in 1654, and he
survived until 1673. His children, all of whom married, were Thomas, Joane, Elizabeth, Mary, Josiah,
Sarah, and Hannah. Mary, the authoress, was born
in England. She married the Reverend Joseph Rowlandson in 1656. The dates of her birth, her marriage,
and her death are not found recorded. She had four
children, born in Lancaster: Mary, 1657; died 1660;
Joseph, 1661; died 1713 in Weathersfield, having a
son Wilson; Mary, 1665; married Jonathan Blodget,
of Salisbury; Sarah, 1669; died of a wound while a
captive at New Braintree, February 29, 1675/6.

THE DESTRUCTION OF LANCASTER. A brief outline
of the tragedy at Lancaster, February 10, 1675/6,
supplying some details not given by Mrs. Rowlandson, is needful to a full understanding of her story.

The heroic warrior, James Wiser, a Christian con-
vert of the Nashaway tribe, employed as a scout by

Governor Leverett, on January 24, 1675/6, brought timely notice that the hostile Indians assembled near Quabaug (North Brookfield) would fall upon the English settlements in twenty days, and that they would first assault Lancaster, then a frontier town of about fifty families, organized into five or six garrisons. The colonial authorities failed to recognize the importance of the warning. But another daring scout dragged himself to Major Gookin's door in Cambridge a little before midnight on February 9, exhausted with his eighty-mile journey through the wilderness upon snow-shoes from Menameset (New Braintree), bringing complete confirmation of Wiser's report. The confederate tribes were on the warpath, and the blow was to fall on the morrow. Major Gookin hurriedly despatched a messenger to Concord and Marlborough, ordering the military companies there to the assistance of Lancaster. At Marlborough, Captain Samuel Wadsworth was posted with about forty men. Upon receipt of the message at daybreak, he hastened with his command to the already beleaguered town about ten miles distant, and, by good fortune evading an ambuscade, fought his way to the garrison house of Cyprian Stevens, which was near and in sight of the Rowlandson home, but across the river.

Rumors of the threatening tempest of savage wrath had stirred the quietude of the Nashaway Valley, and the minister, Joseph Rowlandson, with the chief military officer of the town, Lieutenant Henry Kerley, and other leading citizens, had gone to the Bay to beg help from the Council. There were probably fourteen or more soldiers from the lower towns detailed among the various Lancaster garrisons. Wadsworth's force was insufficient for aggressive tactics, and his arrival too late to assist those in the minister's garrison. At John Prescott's, Richard Wheeler's, Thomas Sawyer's, and Nathaniel Joslin's, as well as Cyprian Stevens' palisaded houses, the defense was successful, and the Indians, knowing that a mounted force of eighty men from Concord and other reënforcements were approaching, retired to the hills with rich spoils gathered from abandoned farms and twenty-four captives; where they were safe from any force the English could bring against them. In a single day a fair scene of rural industry and content had become more desolate than the rude wilderness from which it had been laboriously conquered.

The survivors under the protection of the soldiers buried their mangled dead, and such as had no relatives in the Bay towns able to receive them were gathered into the well-fortified garrison of Thomas Sawyer in the south village and that of Cyprian Stevens near the North River Bridge.

On March 26, troopers and carts sent for the purpose by Major Simon Willard removed the people and their chattels to Concord, and the wolves and savages resumed their sovereignty along the Nashua. The Lancaster families in their banishment were scattered far and wide wherever they could find friendly shelter. By various local records of births and deaths among

them between 1676 and 1680, when many of them re-
turned to their dearly bought lands in the valley, we
know that the Prescotts, Hudsons, and some of the
Sawyers were at Concord; the Wilders, Willards,
Houghtons, Waters, and Ropers, in Charlestown; the
Farrars, at Woburn; the Whitcombs, at Scituate; the
Lewises, Bemans, Rogers, Sumners, and Athertons,
at Dorchester. The Rowlandsons removed from
Boston to Wethersfield, Connecticut, in the spring of
1677. (Abridged from the notes of the 1903 edition of
Mr. Henry Stedman Nourse and Colonel John Eliot
Thayer.)